Career
Confidence

ROBYNN STOREY

CEO of Storeyline Resumes

Career Confidence

No-BS Stories & Strategies for Finding Your Power

WILEY

For general information on our other products and services or for technical support, please contact our Customer Care Department within the United States at (800) 762-2974, outside the United States at (317) 572-3993 or fax (317) 572-4002.

Wiley also publishes its books in a variety of electronic formats. Some content that appears in print may not be available in electronic formats. For more information about Wiley products, visit our web site at www.wiley.com.

Library of Congress Cataloging-in-Publication Data is Available:

ISBN 9781394219988 (Cloth)
ISBN 9781394220922 (ePub)
ISBN 9781394220915 (ePDF)

Cover Art and Design: Paul Mccarthy

SKY10071461_040124

For Alexa and Jack. You are the loves of my life, my laughter, my joy, my pride, and my heart.

For my beloved husband, Chris, the most steadfast anchor in my life, the solid rock upon which our family has been built, and undeniably, the funniest guy I have ever known.

Contents

Acknowledgments

Thank you to my children, Alexa and Jack. You are the loves of my life, my laughter, my joy, my pride and my heart. Each day as your mother has been a blessing and an honor. Watching you grow and thrive has been an honor beyond words, a privilege I cherish with all of my being. You both continually astound me with your kindness, your intelligence, and your remarkable ability to find beauty and goodness in the world around you. I love you both with a love that knows no bounds, a love that will forever flow, unending. You are my greatest blessings, my most cherished gifts, and the source of the purest joy in my life.

Thank you to my husband, Chris, for being the unwavering force that has steadied my ship through life's unpredictable waters. Your infectious sense of humor has filled our days with laughter and warmth, making every moment we share a treasure. I am eternally grateful for your spirit, always ready to embrace new adventures and seize every opportunity that comes our way. Here's to a future filled with more laughter, love, and shared adventures.

My parents, Bob and Sandy Sofranko, provided the basis of my happiest childhood memories, and who live the Mr. Rogers's way of life, every single day. You have always been and will always be the most kind, loving, supportive and wonderful people I've ever known.

My grandparents, Sam and Fran Vecchio, set the bar high for love, laughter, and happiness.

My beautiful, artistic, brilliant, and wonderful big sister, Louisa Wotus, who talks the talk and walks the walk. Your belief in faith, family, and community is an inspiration to everyone around you, especially me.

To my best friends, Janet and Anita, we shared a whole lifetime of raising kids, feeding the neighborhood, and justifying our excessive purchases of clothes, shoes, and candles. Thank you for always being there for me.

To my fun squad, Grace Otto DiScienzo and Peter DiScienzo. Though you may not officially be "my children," in my heart, you hold a cherished place as my own. Your presence in my life has brought an abundance of joy, laughter, fun, and car-ride sing-alongs that shall continue to go unrecorded.

To my team at Storeyline Resumes, all the wonderfully talented professionals who make up our business. Thank you for your talent, dedication, and passion for helping our clients tell their best professional stories.

I would like to thank all the people at Wiley who have helped me along this journey, specifically my editor, Julie Kerr, and Leah Zarra, my acquisitions editor. Thank you for believing that I had something to say. I could never have done this without your incredible knowledge and support.

And, to all the hundreds of thousands of customers who trusted us to help them pave their professional path, for sharing their inspirational journeys and keeping me armed with a zillion stories of perseverance, success, and self-worth.

Introduction

Hi! I am Robynn Storey. The author of this book.

This book is about resumes. Yep, another book about resumes.

This book is also NOT about resumes. It is about a resume business. And the extraordinary people I've met along the way.

Didn't know a resume business was a thing? It is.

A pretty big one.

A little about me. I grew up as a poor kid in a rural small town in Pennsylvania. My biggest ambition in life was to get OUT of said small town, but with no money, no resources, and parents who wanted me to go to college, get married, and make babies, my dreams of heading to New York City or Los Angeles were stalled before they started.

So, I did all the things I was supposed to do. I became a good student, a good person, a wife and a mother at a very young age. With two, count 'em, two marriages under my belt by the age of 24, I longed for adventure, a different kind of life, excitement, and something more than just enough money to pay the rent.

By the time I turned 30, I'd done pretty well for myself. A few corporate roles, a few big titles, and a six-figure paycheck. You'd think I'd be happy. I wasn't. I threw it all away after a crazy day of mommy guilt when I, yet again, had to pack up two kids before dawn so I could attend another meaningless morning meeting.

So, what does a responsible wife and mother do? She tosses it all in the trash, burns it down, and gives up a semi-comfortable life to become a waitress. And resume writer.

In the 23 years since I founded Storeyline Resumes, we have worked with hundreds of thousands of customers to develop their resume packages, tell their stories, and help THEM achieve their goals.

I've seen incredible success, inspirational evolutions, heartbreak, sadness, and victory . . . all through the eyes and stories of the clients we've met along the way.

This book is about them, their stories, and their lives. And it's also about how I started off making nothing and grew this business to $10 million annually by caring about other people and encouraging them to beat down every door, take every opportunity, and push themselves beyond their capabilities to get paid what they are worth.

I am so glad you are joining me on this journey; hope you have a few laughs, learn something new, and adapt your own career path as you read about things like resumes, finding your way, when you should take chances, how to deal with bad jobs, how to find a good one, and most importantly, how something you are going through or have gone through in your career is reflected in these stories I'll be telling. I hope you find solutions, inspiration, or ideas to carve out your career path. It's a fun ride, so read on!

1

Life's a Gamble

My grandfather was a bookie.

For anyone who doesn't know what that is, he took bets on numbers, sports, and a variety of other chance games.

He was not big time. Most bets were done in the form of nickels and dimes.

His customers were mostly poor people who were throwing their coins into the proverbial fountain, hoping to come out with a few extra dollars.

Which is funny because he was poor too.

His day job was working in a factory where they made tennis balls. And on nights and weekends, he bartended and waited tables at our hometown Italian restaurant.

On Saturday mornings we would go around and pick up money. Then he would go to the bank, deposit the loot into a safety deposit box, and then he'd take me and my sister for ice cream.

At the time, I had no idea what was going on, but I knew that Saturday mornings were fun, and the people we visited often had treats for us.

Do you remember the line from *Goodfellas* where Karen says something to the effect of: "Other men were sitting around every day waiting for handouts from their bosses at the end of the month.

Mobsters were different. They went out every day and came back with money."

It was like that, but without the violence and the huge stacks of cash.

All I know is that my grandfather was a hustler. Any job, any opportunity to make money, any work hours, requests, side gigs were always met with a resounding "yes."

My earliest memories from childhood include picking up cash and playing cards for money. We played scat for nickels, which graduated to blackjack and poker. Some days I would leave the games with bags full of nickels and dimes; other days, I'd leave with empty pockets.

Either way, the excitement of the game held my attention, and as I got older, I craved higher and higher stakes.

I am a gambler to this day. Love the action of the casino, love the win, don't mind the loss.

I am also a gambler in life. Willing to take a chance, throw caution to the wind, bet on myself and others.

Sometimes you win; sometimes you lose.

I find that the most successful people do not focus on money. Sure, that's ultimately the end goal for many people, but for most entrepreneurs, me included, it is the thrill of the game.

The people willing to gamble, quit their jobs to do something new, take a job that is beyond their current capabilities, or start a business with no idea of how they will pay the mortgage, often become the most successful people.

They are the hustlers.

They trade in passion.

And sometimes they beat the house.

For my grandfather, all I know is that his efforts allowed them to pay for cars in cash.

Once he bought my grandma a fur coat. No one we knew had a fur coat.

We had the extras that most people in our neighborhood did not, and that, come Christmas time, presents for me and my sister were stacked up to the ceiling when most of our friends got an apple in their stockings and maybe a bike or baseball bat.

By no means am I suggesting you take your life savings and put it all on red.

I am suggesting that taking a chance, in life, in work, in relationships often leads to the greatest wins of all.

> Don't be afraid to bet on yourself.

2

What's in a Name?

My last name is Storey. The name of my business is Storeyline Resumes. It was like the stars, moon, and sun aligned when I married my husband and took his name.

What's the likelihood that my actual last name would reflect what I turned out to do for a living?

I tell people we came up with the name of my business over a cigarette (me) and a beer (my husband). After the kiddos were put to bed, we'd venture out onto the tiny front porch of our first house and hang out, chat, smoke, drink, and dream.

I knew I wanted to be a writer, but I was not interested in writing books (ironic, I know), couldn't make money writing business papers, and while I love all kinds of literature, I am no poet.

Since I had a background in human resources, I knew what hiring managers were looking for, and resumes seemed to be a thing. Everyone needs a resume, right?

So, I started off writing for family and friends. Then they would send THEIR friends to me and on and on and on, until one day, I said, "Hey, I think I can make this a full-time business."

Talking about it now, it seems like it was simple. I can assure you that it was not. We were not in a place financially for me to start a business. I still had to have a job, bring home the bacon, pay the mortgage, the groceries, the bills. Just like everyone else, we couldn't live on love or ramen noodles. Not with four mouths to feed.

So, I continued working my day job, and would write resumes at night. And on the weekends. And in the morning before work. It was a rat race.

I remember once being in an operations meeting at my "real job" and my cell phone rang. It was a resume client. I excused myself from the meeting, walked outside, and took the call.

It was right then and there that I knew I was WAAAAY more excited to be doing resumes than being a HR manager. So, I talked to my husband, and we brainstormed to find a way for me to jump in. Both feet. He said, "If you can do something to cover the groceries, I can float us for a bit on the rest of the bills."

Done. I agreed. I gave up my job and started waiting tables. I worked during the day to build my business, take care of the kids, cook, clean, grocery shop, and all the things you have to do, and at night, I waitressed.

I was a terrible waitress.

I cannot walk 10 feet without tripping over lint, so carrying heavy trays was quite the challenge. My first week, I dropped an entire tray of glasses. I also spilled a full glass of red wine on a businessman in a white shirt and blue suit. He was not amused, nor did he care that I was a fledgling entrepreneur.

Thank goodness the owner of the restaurant was a friend of a friend, and they gave me another chance. I learned how to carry the trays. Sometimes I just brought out meals by the plate. I was always willing to work the banquet, work the wedding, work the weekends, work the parties, graduations, anniversaries, and any other event they had.

I stashed one-dollar bills into a shoe box like a stripper stashes them in her G-string. Little by little, I made enough money to pay what needed to be paid, and within a year, I gave up being a terrible waitress and became a full-time writer.

The first year of full-time resume writing I made $30,000.

In 2022, my business made nearly $10 million dollars in revenue.

So, see? It's super easy to be an entrepreneur. You just have to dedicate all of your waking hours to your business and spend

20+ years crafting your trade. And skip vacations, days off, sleep, sanity, and meals.

The first major breakthrough in the business happened when the housing bubble burst of 2008. I was approached by a mortgage company to write nearly 90 resume packages for their key management team that were going to lose their jobs. After weeks and weeks of working around the clock to interview each client, create resumes, and cover letters, I realized I could no longer go it alone, and finally hired my first writer to join my team. He was a comedy writer named Will. He had never written resumes; he wrote scripts for sitcom television. But I needed a writer, and he needed a job. Turns out, he was an amazing writer, and since he specialized in comedy, he kept me laughing the entire time he was with me.

Since then, we've added 60+ people to our team. Some have been here 10 or 15 years, some 5 or 8, and some are new. But when you care about people, pay them fairly, treat them with dignity, respect, and care, they stay.

They are happy. Happy to be part of something fun, fulfilling, and lucrative. Plus, since Will, we only hire people with a sense of humor. In a high-stress job like ours, you have to be able to give a laugh and have a laugh.

And that's my Storey.

But it wasn't always. My maiden name is Sofranko and my family name is Vecchio. I've always been so proud of my Italian and European heritage, and obviously marrying someone with a cool last name has been a bonus for me. But what if your name is hard to pronounce? Or you are a foreigner in a strange land?

I once worked with a client by the name of Michael. He was an information technology executive for a huge Fortune 500 company. When I got on the phone to interview him, he had a very strong Indian accent. An incredibly friendly and knowledgeable guy, I asked him how he got the name "Michael."

"My name is Mohammed," he told me, but when he came to work in America, his boss suggested that he simplify his name to "Michael."

I was appalled and did not hold back. He laughed and said it was no big deal. His arrival in the United States was shortly after 9/11 and being named Mohammed, he said, was not something he wanted to deal with. He was already struggling to keep up with his fast-talking American peers, and desperately wanted to "fit in."

After I did a bit of research, I found it was fairly common practice in the 1990s and 2000s to "Americanize" the names of new immigrants or VISA employees so that it was easier for them to engage, and easier for their counterparts to pronounce their names.

For the record, this is not a practice I agree with. How hard is it to learn to pronounce someone's name? Are we that arrogant to suggest your name makes our life difficult?

Your name is an integral part of your identity. It carries your heritage, culture, and family history. Changing it to fit into a new environment can lead to a sense of inauthenticity. Instead, embrace your cultural background and educate your peers on how to pronounce it. Your distinct experiences and perspectives are valuable assets.

By adopting an American-sounding name, you inadvertently discourage your colleagues from learning about and appreciating your culture. Diversity in the workplace is not just about physical appearances. It's about the rich tapestry of traditions, languages, and perspectives that different cultures bring. In today's world, asking African American women to not wear their natural hair, or discouraging our Islamic friends from wearing their head coverings would be—should be—met with outrage. It just shouldn't be done. Plus, who doesn't love learning about different cultures and traditions?

If you change your name, it can lead to confusion because your official employment records and documents do not match your workplace persona, leading to misunderstandings and complications. So, it's my advice that instead of changing your name, take pride in your cultural heritage. Educate your colleagues about your background, traditions, and language. Be an advocate for diversity and inclusion, and you might inspire others to do the same.

> Embrace the power of your name, for it carries the essence of your unique journey and the potential to shape your destiny.

3 | How Did We Get Here?

If you were born in the 1970s, 1980s, or even the early part of the 1990s, looking for a job was like a little exercise in nepotism, dumb luck, and the right place, right time.

Everyone who wanted a job, for the most part, had a job.

Most of us got jobs because we knew someone who worked at a company we were interested in, or we met someone in college whose parents worked for a company. We sent out some resumes, LinkedIn didn't exist, and job boards were not a thing.

We typed, printed, and mailed our resumes to job opportunities we saw in the newspaper, or later, online.

Unemployment ranged from 5% to 7%, give or take a few tenths of a percentage, and finding a job was, well, pretty easy. It may not have been the exact job you wanted, but if you needed one, you filled out an application, a nice HR lady gave you a call, and boom, you went to the interview.

If you did not get a job offer, they sent you a postcard in the mail, or called you on the phone and let you know you were not selected. It was all very civilized. It was extremely rare to be ignored, and sometimes, they even kept your resume around, so if another job came up, they called you.

My first grown-up job, a marketing representative for a large local grocery store chain, came about because the father of my best friend was an executive there.

After graduating from college with a degree in communication and marketing, it was fair to say that I knew almost nothing about communications or marketing.

What I did have was a passion for learning, a passion for paying my rent, and a passion for shoes. These things cannot be had without a job. I did not know one single person who had parents who paid their rent or bought them food or supported them in any way. Once you graduated from high school or college, you were expected to be out of the house. That's just how things worked. And YOU wanted to be out of the house. There was nothing I wanted more than some privacy and independence. So, off we all went.

I did not make the first cut at the grocery store chain. The company hired someone else. Even though I was highly unqualified, had no real knowledge of the grocery business, and zero experience in doing anything other than making ice cream cones (which I acquired at my college job), I was super cute and bubbly and friendly. Alas, that was not enough for them . . . so, they passed. I went on to keep in touch with the hiring manager, took a job at a bank doing customer service and sales, and a year later, the store called me back and offered me the position. It paid $26,000 a year. I honestly did not know how I was going to spend all that money.

Hard work has never been and will never be a dirty term for me. The only way to get where you want to go is to work your ass off.

Don't let anyone tell you differently.

I had a friend who graduated with a degree in nuclear engineering from Penn State. He was having a tough time finding a job. It was the 1980s and the recession was in full swing. So, he got a job washing dishes at our hometown Italian restaurant. Every night, six days a week, this brilliant young engineer scrubbed pots and pans, dishes, and glasses over a sink steaming with hot water and soap, just to make minimum wage and a free plate of spaghetti at the end of his shift.

He did this for two years. No one said, "You are too good for that job." No one said, "Here is some money to hold you over until you get a real job." No one asked, "Is your mental health okay? Do you need a break?"

It just wasn't done. If you needed money, you worked. We had no handouts, no backup, no trust funds.

He eventually got a job at Westinghouse. He stayed there his entire career.

Not long ago, I dropped $1,000 into my son's checking account. He's 24. He is "finding himself" right now, waiting tables, going to the gym, hanging out with friends. If, at the age of 24, I told my dad I needed money to support me while "I found myself," he'd still be laughing 30 years later.

Of course, I don't want my son to starve, but I don't want him to expect that life is like this either.

Are we doing our kids a disservice by trying to make everything easy?

My answer is 100% "yes." I am guilty of it, and you probably are too.

Everyone is "triggered" or "offended" by everything these days. Backbone is not something you are born with; it is something you have to earn.

While our children aren't walking to school in the driving snow and blinding rain like our grandparents were, if they were lucky enough to get to school, there are different kinds of challenges.

Along with the prevalence of illegal drugs, partisan political agendas, social media's pressure on kids to be perfect, endless bullying, societal aggression, continuing gun violence, and academic struggles and debates, throw in a global pandemic for good measure, and see that kids today are struggling. Is that bad?

"Yes" and "no."

Most of us have learned how to "adult" by learning how to struggle. Ramen noodles for dinner more nights than not. Staying in instead of going out. Buying a car you could afford instead of the one you really wanted. Going to the beach for a long weekend instead of going to Europe.

We need to not only recognize that our kids are faced with issues we never had to deal with; it is, in fact, their reality. So instead of sentimentalizing the way things "used to be," we need to be figuring out a way to help our kids based on the "way things are."

First, we need to be honest about happiness. What makes one person happy, doesn't necessarily make someone else happy. Some of the most miserable people in the world, who seemingly have it "all" are unhappy. Yet, others who don't measure up to our standards of perfection are content, love their life, and live a joyful existence.

So, where is the balance? First of all, we need to stop making everything look so "easy." Most of the successful people I know have made crazy sacrifices to get to where they are. Me included. At one point, I did not take a full vacation for nine years. Yes, I took a day or two here and there, but it was rare. I worked during the day, worked at night, worked on the weekends. In college, I held three or four jobs at a time.

Don't be afraid to make your kids work, babysit, or cut grass for money when they are young. Earning your own money is a prideful thing. Every college student should have a part-time job or do internships while at school. This allows them to not rely solely on overextended parents for spending money, and it also lets them see what the "real world" is like outside the walls of their campus.

Both my kids worked from the time they were 15 or 16. Could I have paid for their clothes, gas, entertainment? Of course, but when you earn it, it is that much sweeter.

Be honest with your kids about struggle, achievement, performance, and rewards. We live in a "participation trophy" society. While I think it is great to acknowledge someone's hard work and effort, not everyone wins. Games have winners and losers. The best thing you can do for your kids is to let them lose from time to time. It makes it all the sweeter when they win. On their own.

Today, if you are on social media, everyone's life looks a hell of a lot more exciting than yours. It's all a lie. Don't buy it.

There is nothing wrong with work. THAT is what we need to be teaching our kids. Let them pick themselves up when they fall.

Kids are struggling with the balance between what they see online and the lives they are living, which are not always easy or glamorous. Young minds can have a difficult time differentiating between what is real and what is not. As a society, as parents, bosses, coaches, peers, and teachers, I believe the greatest thing we can do for kids today is to not coddle them, but let them win and lose based on their own merits. We are all responsible for shaping young minds, and teaching work ethic through our own actions can help them to understand how fulfilling life can be when you accomplish things on your own.

I've seen a major change in work ethic over my 23 years in this business. We've gone from a society of hustlers, movers, workers, and innovators to wanting four-day work weeks and for everything to be easy.

Life is not easy. Nothing worth having is.

> Your life can be exactly what you want it to be.

4 | A Guy Walks into a Bar

A young man graduates from college with no idea of what he wants to do with his life. I will call him John.

John can't find a professional job. He leaves school without any real-life skills. Beer pong champion does not count. He has student loans, wants to move out of his parents' house and mostly wants to get laid, go to bars, and hang out with his friends.

So he gets a job at the mall, at a well-known department store.

He starts off working in the stock room. He unloads boxes from trucks. He sorts and takes clothing out of plastic wrap, puts them on hangers, puts those on racks, and takes them to the sales floor to be displayed by the retail workers.

John does this, day in, day out, for two years. He never calls off. He is always pleasant. And he's picked up a few fashion tips from looking at "almost" designer clothes for those two years.

One day, a woman from the company's corporate office comes to the store for a visit. You know this kind of visit: "We realize you are peons, and that you barely make minimum wage, but I am here to tell you how important you are to our company before I drive off in my Mercedes and never think of you again."

As she makes her trip around the store, she spots this young (well-dressed for the stock-room job) man and strikes up a conversation. It helps that he's pretty cute. And very friendly.

They chat. She asks him about himself. He talks about his work and how much he likes the company and would like to "do something else." She asks him if he's ever thought about being a buyer. He truthfully tells her that he doesn't even know what that is, but if it can get him out of the stock room, he's in.

So, the company promotes him into a junior buyer position and for four years he learns about fashion trends, accessories, how to spot the next big thing, and how to plan, source, buy, and select items to be sold in its stores.

He's affable. He's handsome. He's a quick learner. Before you know it, he's running all the buying for the men's department for their 500+ U.S. stores.

Years (and many promotions) later, John is in New York City for Fashion Week. After a long day of schmoozing, catwalk watching, and air kisses, he heads to a bar in lower Manhattan to get a drink.

He sidles up to the bar, orders a drink, and takes a seat. After a few cocktails, he starts to chat with a gentleman seated next to him. They talk about their drinks, what they are going to have for dinner, the weather, and a variety of other things. They hit it off.

So, he introduces himself to his bar mate, tells him he is in New York City for Fashion Week and that he runs buying for several divisions of a major department store. The guy tells him he is also there for Fashion Week, and then they proceed to chat about that.

As they leave, the guy hands John his business card and says, "If you'd ever consider coming to work for a designer, give me a call." John, boozed up on a few too many drinks, takes the card, shoves it in his pocket, and shakes the guy's hand.

The next day, John pulls the card out of his pocket. He is stunned. It is the business card of one of the most famous, most successful designers in the United States.

He flies home, calls the guy, and never looks back. By the time John comes to Storeyline Resumes, he's already spent nearly a decade with the famous designer and has moved on to ANOTHER famous designer (when I spoke to him, he had just spent hours in her Long Island home doing yoga and negotiating the sale of one her "intimates" lines to a new buyer).

He was ready to move on, do something international, and we worked with him on his resume package to get him prepared for a pretty easy job search.

The moral of the story? Always talk to people in bars. You just never know where your next opportunity is going to come from.

> Always be on the lookout for new friends, new connections, and new opportunities; people have landed jobs because of someone they talked to in an elevator, airplane, or bar.

5

There Is Nothing Wrong with You

I am the youngest in my family. I have an older sister and my mom is an only child. To say we were the center of the universe would be an understatement. We were doted on, spoiled by our grandparents, and every little thing we did was met with exuberance and praise. Got an *A* on the spelling test? It's time for cake! Came in second place in the softball tournament? Let's have a party to celebrate!

My sister and I would make up little plays and musicals, and at parties, we would "perform" them. Everyone would cheer, and laugh, and tell us how smart and beautiful and talented we were.

I went to Catholic school from first grade to eighth grade. I was with the same group of 20 kids all those years. The teachers were kind; we felt comfortable with each other, bullying was not a thing, and going to church every school morning (and once on the weekends) kept us all on our best behavior.

When I started first grade (there was no kindergarten back then), my first teacher was a nun. Her name was Sister Evangeline. She was about 4-foot-10-inches tall and dressed in the traditional nun habit. She smelled like roses and was the sweetest human being I've ever met.

Every morning, she'd line us all up in the hallway and hug us good morning. And at the end of the school day, she'd do the same and give us a blessing for a safe school bus trip home.

I always felt loved, protected, and insulated from the world around me.

My parents were poor. To afford the Catholic school tuition, the parish would pay half, and the parents formed a group and had non-stop fundraisers to pay the other half. So, our summers were spent hosting church bingo, serving pizzas, and raising funds for tuition. We had church festivals, bake sales, and garage sales—the proceeds of which all went to pay for our tuition.

But little by little, our group of hometown Catholic school students became fewer and fewer in number. The parents were tired of fundraising, public school was free, so by the time I went to eighth grade, there were only six kids left in the group. And then the church announced that they were no longer paying half the tuition, so it was impossible for my parents to afford the cost of the Catholic high school.

So, in ninth grade, I had to go to public high school. I went from catching the bus at 8 a.m. to catching the bus at 6 a.m. And that was only the beginning of the changes I experienced.

I had spent my life feeling confident about whom I was, what I was supposed to be doing, and why people liked me. I was raised to be a good girl. I did not question any authority and followed the rules like the good Italian Catholic girl that I was. No one was ever really mean to me. No one ever made fun of me.

Of all my friends, no one had more of anything or less of anything. We were all poor and there was not a single one of my friends whose parents were divorced. No one did drugs. No one had a drinking habit; our parents rarely swore, other than the occasional "shit" or "damn," and to this day, I've never heard either of my parents say the "f" word.

Ninth grade marked the juncture where my life took a tumultuous turn. With a heart brimming with confidence, I entered the public high school, decked out in my best attire—a pair of Sears and Roebuck jeans, no-name sneakers, and a vivid pink top snagged on sale. However, my dreams of a triumphant debut were quickly shattered.

When I arrived at school, the first thing I did was get lost. I had no idea how to navigate the giant circular building that housed both the middle school and high schools.

I was late for my first class, which turned out to be on the other side of the building, and I was carrying my backpack and lunch with me because I could not figure out how to unlock the lock to my locker. In Catholic school, we had little cubbies. Nothing was locked up.

It was probably 90 degrees outside that early September day, and by the time I arrived to my English class, I was a hot, sweaty, nervous mess. It did not help matters when the teacher said "Miss Sofranko (my maiden name), you are late. Find a seat."

She did not hug me. Or wish me a good day.

I spotted a seat at the back of the room, tripped over my untied shoelaces, and slid into the desk where I prayed no one saw me trip.

My hands were shaking as I tried to quietly find my pencil. I opened my Hello Kitty notebook while a group of much more seasoned, much more confident, and much more COOL classmates stared and snickered.

Welcome to the ninth grade!

After the bell rang, I rushed to the girls' bathroom where I hid in a stall and bawled my eyes out. I was mortified. Embarrassed. I desperately wanted to call my mom to pick me up, but we only had one car and my dad was at work. I could not believe this was going to be my life.

I struggled through the rest of the day, and the only person I talked to was my sister, who thankfully was kind enough not to ignore me when we passed in the hallway.

Things went from bad to worse. I dreaded school every single day. I could not seem to make friends. The kids in public school were more sophisticated, much cooler, and they had known each other their whole lives. I did not fit in.

Around Thanksgiving of that year, I was sitting in my biology class and a pretty, dark-haired girl walked into class. She was new.

Her family had just moved here from New York City and her name was Laura. The seat next to me was empty and when she sat down, our eyes met and I said, "Hello."

That day, we sat together at lunch. I was used to sitting by myself or trying to find a seat in the cafeteria with the other outcasts, so it was nice to finally sit with someone whom I could chat with.

Our school was in the heart of rural western Pennsylvania, and I had never met someone from New York City before. She was Italian Catholic, like me, and she also stood out like a sore thumb, just like me.

We became fast friends. She was sweet, funny, a little shy, and also unsure of how to navigate our new realities. So, we stuck together like glue, visited each other's houses, and hers was the first place I'd ever stayed overnight other than my own home.

Her mom and dad, both Italians, just like me, became my second home. I loved them, they loved me, and always made me feel welcome. Little by little, my and Laura's friendship helped us both to become a bit more confident, a bit surer of ourselves, and a bit more comfortable making other friends. So, we expanded our friend circle, and by the time tenth grade rolled around, I was no longer a hot miserable mess and that was all thanks to her.

As a footnote, you remember how I mentioned a friend's dad recommended me for my first job? It was Laura's dad. He was an executive at a local grocery store chain, and when I graduated college and got my first "real job," he was the one who recommended me and vouched for me.

So, what is the moral of this story? Well, for the first time in my life, I struggled with my identity. I was used to having lots of friends, being well liked and accepted. But the change from Catholic school to public school was a rough one.

I kept wondering, what the hell was wrong with me?

The answer? Nothing, really, other than being different. In retrospect, my journey through ninth grade was a lesson in humility. The transition taught me that it's not about what's wrong with me, but about embracing my uniqueness. The struggles and challenges I faced were mere steppingstones on my path to discovering my authentic self.

So, if you don't fit in, aren't getting called for the job you want, or can't seem to find your way, rest assured that there is not a damn thing wrong with you. We don't always, and most of us will never, fit into the mold of whom or what others want us to be. Being true to yourself, your quirks, and your differences will help you to be the best version of what works for you.

> Sometimes, all we need is a bit of an identity crisis to figure out where we belong.

6 | Fake It 'Til You Make It

When I first started off my resume company back in 2000, I was doing it part-time while working a full-time corporate job. So, I would interview resume clients at night, put the kids to bed, and develop the clients' resumes during the late-night hours.

I also worked on the weekends as needed. I did this for a few years, had a website created, and started getting a steady stream of business. I did not have any staff or employees, and did all the work myself. From the marketing to the customer service, to the writing, it was a one-woman show.

As I began to get a bit busier, I hired a writer to join the company. As I previously mentioned, he was a hilarious guy by the name of Will. He was a script writer for comedy sitcoms on television and was looking for some freelance work.

I would talk to the customer, take notes, and send them to Will. He was a night owl as well, and his projects would come back to me in at 3 or 4 in the morning.

It was an arrangement that worked well for both of us. He was super smart, very, very funny, and kept me in stitches those first few lean years.

By the time 2006 rolled around, I jumped feet first into my business, gave up my corporate job, and took a job waiting tables to make enough grocery money to keep us going. By then, I had a husband and two kids, and while it may seem romantic to throw yourself into an entrepreneurial venture, where you've escaped the corporate rat race, kids don't care about that. They would like to eat and get new shoes. So, I did what I needed to do to make sure they had more than frozen waffles for dinner.

I worked on resumes and business development during the day while the kids were at school, and when my husband came home from work, I went off to my waitressing job.

I don't think I made more than $5,000 or $6,000 a year writing resumes those first few years.

That all changed in 2008 when the mortgage bubble burst and the bottom fell out of the U.S. economy. Banks, finance, mortgage companies, and corporations across the spectrum began shedding jobs with an absolute ferocity not seen since the dot.com bust of 2001.

At the beginning of 2007, unemployment was at 5%. By the end of 2009, it was 10%. Home prices fell by 30% over the course of 24 months, and the subprime mortgage industry went belly-up.

If you don't know what subprime mortgages are, they are basically mortgages that allowed borrowers to borrow WAY more money than they could actually pay back. Some mortgages would give you upfront monies to buy a bigger house than you could afford, and in a few years, the interest rates ballooned from 4% or 5% to 20% or more. So basically, a subprime mortgage was giving you the opportunity to have your champagne dream house on your beer money budget.

For a generation of young people and homebuyers, that meant you could get the new house of your dreams, one bigger than your parents lived in, but you would not be able to afford much of anything else once the higher payments kicked in.

My husband and I built a house during that time. Between the two of us, we were making around $125,000 a year. I was only working part time, and my husband, an accountant, brought in the majority of our income.

We got approved for a $600,000 mortgage. Smartly, and despite my nagging for a 6,000-square-foot house, an in-ground pool, and hardwood floors, we only built a house for $200,000.

My new neighbors? Not so much. We were the only family who could put in a concrete driveway and went on vacation that year, while my neighbors in our new subdivision could not afford to buy dining room furniture until their toddlers went to college.

So basically, everyone was given the option for loans they simply could not afford, and when hundreds of thousands of people couldn't make their mortgage payments, the shit hit the fan.

So, sometime around the middle of 2008, most subprime lenders in the United States were failing. One such lender had over 500 U.S.-based offices and it was leaving the market for greener (and less restrictive) international pastures.

I received a phone call from one of these branches and talked to a very young executive who asked me if I could write some resume packages for a few of their employees who were going to be losing their jobs.

Before my brain could ask too many intelligent questions, I agreed. Turns out, they needed 89 of them. That's right: 89 resume packages. They all needed to be done within six weeks so these people could look for new jobs.

If I had thought too long and hard about it, I would have said "no." There is no way this could be done. But I didn't. I said "yes," and jumped in with both feet.

It was at that moment that "fake it 'til you make it" flashed through my brain, and I was determined that no matter what, I could do it.

I interviewed 89 people, sometimes in the middle of the night to accommodate time differences. I worked on the weekends, I worked nonstop and developed full resume packages. Over those six weeks, I made about $30,000, more than I'd previously made in the last few years combined.

Would I recommend it? Yes, and no. I was exhausted and brain dead trying to think of 89 individual things to say about 89 people who were basically doing the same job. But what I showed myself and my clients was that I could handle the pressure, do great work, and help my clients tell their best professional stories. But, long term, that was not a sustainable business model. But the experience helped me figure out that if I wanted to do this work, build this business, I would need other people. And so that's what I did. I hired writers, my first interviewers, and an admin to answer the phones, handle emails, and keep us afloat.

If I had never said "yes" and adopted my "fake it 'til you make it attitude," I'd probably still be doing four or five resumes a week, instead of working with the 200+ clients that we work with today.

A few years ago, we were working with a youngish (mid-thirties) client who was managing warehousing operations for a small manufacturing company. He was managing everything from staffing to safety to day-to-day operations, and doing a really great job. His salary was $80,000 a year, which is pretty normal for the type of operation he was handling.

But during and after the pandemic, the supply chain, warehousing, and distribution industries was a bit of a mess, and companies were looking for people to help them figure out how to fulfill all the orders from an entire world that was laying on the couch, watching Netflix, and ordering stuff they did not need from their phones.

So, after we did his resume and LinkedIn profile, he was ready to take advantage of some of the hiring opportunities he'd seen in his industry.

A few weeks later, he called me to say he was interviewing for a job with a much larger company, and the position would entail him managing three large distribution centers. It was a much bigger job; he'd go from leading a team of under 100 people to leading a team of over 600. The salary would move him from $80,000 a year to $175,000 a year.

That was an enormous jump, and he was justifiably nervous. "I don't think I can do it," he said. "I feel like I am going to be in over my head and I will probably fail."

I shared with him my "fake it 'til you make it" philosophy.

I asked him. . .

What's the worst thing that could happen?

Do you want to make more money?

Could you learn the company's technology, apply your experience to a bigger team, and act confident even if you did not feel so confident?

His answer: "yes." And the worst thing that could happen is that he could crash and burn, but he'd be doing it in a time when jobs in his industry were a dime a dozen.

He took the job, and I have not heard from him since. I assume he's doing well because he has not called us to update his resume.

So, if you have been lucky enough to have been presented with an opportunity that you feel is above your pay grade, or will stretch your talent or capabilities, say "yes." The worst thing that can happen is that you will fail. The best thing, and the thing most likely to happen, is that you will succeed.

> Saying "yes" instead of "no" can help you take your career to new heights.

7 | Want Loyalty? Get a Dog.

During the 1970s and 1980s, the prevailing theme in employment was something called "lifelong employment."

Nearly every dad I knew had a job at a company where he worked from the time he graduated from high school, got out of the military, or graduated from college. It was not an oddity for someone to work at one company their entire life.

Let that sink in. One company, for 40 or 50 years.

Retirement, pensions, annual wage increases, vacation time, annual family picnics, a week or two off between Christmas and New Year's was the norm.

My dad worked at a Volkswagen factory, and they changed the equipment for their annual new car models starting the week after Thanksgiving. So, he was off for 6 weeks at the end of the year. Every year. I thought everyone got this six-week break.

Companies invested heavily in their employees. From training to development to matching 401(k) contributions, health insurance benefits (including dental), and in turn, people committed to their companies for the long haul.

There was a sense of pride in working for a company, and in return, the company supported you during personal and professional challenges.

I remember my dad always wearing his Volkswagen hat or sweatshirt, or my friends' dads who worked for Westinghouse, Kennametal, or the Elliot Company were always in their hats or T-shirts too. And based on the stories I heard, work was fun. They liked their peers, were always joking around, playing gags on each other, and I remember my mom baking cookies or cupcakes every week for my dad to take to work. Everyone did that. They were like a family.

During the summers, my dad's work buddies would come over for cookouts, and once a year, all the families would get together for the annual company picnic. It was usually at a park, amusement park, or public pool. The employers would have games for the kids, they would hand out prizes, and of course, everything was paid for by the company. Some summers, those picnics were the highlight of my summer vacation.

If anyone got fired, it was because they did something heinous. They stole, they abused someone, they repeatedly did not show up for work, and so on. Even then, a lot of laborers belonged to a union, and if you got in trouble, the union stepped in, got your job back, and you got a slap on the wrist.

But times changed, and the world became more fluid. People began moving around; there were more people willing to leave their hometowns to go to work for a company somewhere else, and the dawn of the internet and advances in technology made it easier for us to operate in a global workforce.

Times changed and people changed too, and now, if you have been with your employer for more than 10 years, you are an oddity. How many people can you name who have been with the same company for 20 years or more? Probably not too many.

The loyalty that our parents had to their employers, and those employers with them, seems to have vanished. As companies became more interested in astronomical profits than the people who worked for them, employee loyalty to those companies died.

So, how do you find the balance?

No one wants to work for a company that they don't care about. Most of us want and need to be invested in the products and services we provide or sell. If you are in a job you don't really care about, or employed by a company that doesn't really care about you, you probably are not going to last too long in that job.

We have worked with countless clients who dedicated their lives to their employers. They worked so hard, and so long, and so many hours, that they missed out on their families. Their kids. Their vacations, their time off, their holidays, and their sanity, all in the name of "providing for their families," but they forgot to enjoy those families.

I recently had a client who had worked for her employer for 27 years. She helped the owners start the company, became their first salesperson, grew a huge sales team, and eventually, became its Chief Operating Officer.

They were in the trenches together. They worked hard together. They grew together.

In her last role, she made over \$300,000 a year. And one day, after 27 years, they came in and demoted her. "Times are tough" they said. Their sales were stagnant, and they were looking for ways to cut costs without giving themselves a decrease in their profits.

So, after 27 years, she was the one they chose to save the money on. No mention of the sacrifices she made or the family time she missed, just "you are a liability now, and we need to reduce your salary by \$150,000."

I could tell you hundreds, if not thousands, of stories like this, all heartbreaking, all about people who put in the time, enjoyed the spoils, but were eventually cast out like yesterday's leftovers.

So how do you balance loyalty to yourself and loyalty to your company?

Well, you start off by setting boundaries. If you have a 45-hour workweek, work your 45 hours and be done. While you are working, give it your all, then go home, don't worry about your job, and enjoy your life. If you are off on the weekends, turn off your company cell phone, don't check or respond to emails or texts, and put your out of office response on.

In this world, where we are all connected, all the time, it can be difficult to "shut off," but we must make the effort.

Trust me, answer one email from your boss on a Saturday or Sunday, you'll be expected to answer all emails from your boss on Saturday or Sunday. Respond to a text while you are on vacation? You will be expected to respond to all texts while you are on vacation.

In 2022, I did a LinkedIn post about a client of ours who worked for a tech company, and her experience of going on vacation and her boss's constant communication while she was out of the office. The response I got to this post, the outpouring of similar stories, and the anxiety-ridden response it caused led me to believe that we are a society of people who cannot disconnect. That post, which received over 5 million views and hundreds of thousands likes and comments follows:

After 2 years, 4 months, and 28 days without a day off, a senior account executive for a well-known tech company took her family on vacation.

They went to Disney World.

With three kids under 10, the excitement was at "I can't sleep I am so excited" levels.

Day one: Mom received a call from her boss (right after entering the Magic Kingdom), he needed some info on a client he was meeting in her absence.

Day three: he sent her 11 emails asking questions about accounts/ sales funnels and a client project that was running late.

Day four: he texted her at 6 a.m. and asked her to sit in on a meeting. "It will be short" he told her. It wasn't. She spent 2 hours on a conference call while her family had breakfast without her.

Day six: he texted her around lunch to have a quick chat with him. She replied, "I am on vacation with my family, anything that needs addressed will have to wait until I get back."

Silence. No response. She spent the rest of her vacation with the anxiety about her job hanging over her head.

Upon her return, she gave her two weeks' notice. They asked her to leave that day.

When she came to us to polish up her resume, she was broken and beaten. Mad at herself for not enjoying her time with her family. Mad at herself for not having more "backbone."

After 1 month of job searching, she landed a new job in tech.

Same role, same level, same types of customers.

They have unlimited PTO, WFH options and a boss she likes.

Over the summer, she took a long weekend. She did not receive one call, one text or one email from her boss other than to wish her a "nice long weekend."

Employees have lives.

They have families.

They have well-deserved time away from work.

If you can't respect that, you should not be in charge of people.

This resonates with so many people because we can all see ourselves in this story, especially when we've put an employer first, before ourselves, before our families, before our lives.

So, if you want loyalty, get a dog. If you are looking for it in the workplace, it rarely exists.

> Being loyal to yourself should always come ahead of being loyal to anyone or anything else.

8 | Learned Behavior

Timmy Gianni—April 4, 1957–April 4, 1963

Little Timmy Gianni is buried at our local hometown cemetery.

During the summers, my sister and I spent a lot of time with my grandfather at our local church cemetery. Grandpa went every week to clean the graves, plant flowers, water the plants, and make sure the graves of his siblings, parents, and cousins were all in tip-top shape. My sister and I would go to the old-fashioned well to pump water and drag buckets back to the gravesites of at least 20 or so relatives so they could be watered and cleaned.

I don't know if anyone does this kind of thing anymore, but I have great memories of sunny Saturday mornings planting flowers, talking to my deceased great-grandparents, and strolling around the cemetery, daydreaming about the lives of the people whose names were carved on the tombstones, where they came from, why they died, and who were the people buried on either side of them with the same last names.

My grandpa would point out the young soldiers he knew who perished in WWII, and would tell tales about who was the funniest, the bravest, the ones who left behind wives and kids, the ones who died during their first mission, and the ones who fought bravely and returned home, dying of old age many years later.

He told endless stories about our cousins, aunts, and uncles. My grandma, his wife, was one of 14 children, and one day we found her two little siblings, one boy and one girl, a toddler and an infant, who died during the Spanish influenza.

He seemed to know everyone in that cemetery, where they came from, who they married, how many kids they had, and what those kids did for a living. If I am half the storyteller he was, that would be a generous assumption.

Timmy Gianni is famous in our hometown. He was a 6-year-old boy who had the unfortunate experience of dying on his sixth birthday. He died because he choked to death on a balloon at his own birthday party.

As tragic as this was, his life and death were what we now call a "teachable moment," and every kid I grew up with was carted in front of Timmy's tombstone to learn this lesson.

Balloons are bad.

Our parents and grandparents were so horrified at little Timmy's death that we were told the whole story. How his mom and dad had blown up balloons, how the neighborhood kids were playing hopscotch on the street in front of their house, how the moms were getting the food outside for the lunchtime buffet, how no one really had money to buy birthday presents, so Timmy got homemade gifts and candy from their friends and family.

How the kids got bored and started batting the balloons around, and little Timmy stuck a balloon in his mouth to blow up when he inhaled instead of exhaling. How his dad tried to dislodge the balloon, but in his efforts, just pushed it further down Timmy's throat. How his mother screamed and desperately, desperately smacked his back in the hopes of getting the balloon out. And how the ambulance came 45 minutes later to take Timmy's body to the morgue.

And finally, how the whole town turned up at the funeral to grieve little Timmy, and do what little they could to console his parents.

So, my entire childhood, while filled with birthday parties, there was not one single balloon to be found. Nor do I recall one balloon ever being at a party that I attended for any of my neighborhood friends.

That story is so ingrained in my psyche, that I avoided balloons at my own kids' birthday parties. And if, God forbid, someone had balloons at a party my kids attended, I kept an eagle eye out and strictly forbid them to put any such thing in their mouth.

When they were old enough, I took them to the same cemetery, and told them the same story of Timmy Gianni.

When my daughter's dog turned 4, I had a little present for him. It was a basket filled with dog toys and treats, and a little birthday party kit that I ordered on Amazon to celebrate this little guy.

I know, I know, I am desperate for grandchildren, but for right now, Sunny the Yorkie is what I have. The little kit came with balloons. I blew one up and put it on the little birthday basket. As soon as he came to my house, he tore into his treats. And I popped the balloon with a pair of scissors and threw it in the trash, so he did not try to eat it.

This is learned behavior.

Some life lessons, like little Timmy, stick with us our entire lives. They are things we've heard about, examples that have been set for us, experiences that have changed us, or scared us, or shaped us into whom we are.

So, what does any of this have to do with you and your job search? Plenty.

Let's look at it this way. If your parents went to college, you most likely were encouraged to go to college too. If your mom or dad is an executive, you most likely want to grow up to be an executive too. If your mom or dad was a garbage collector, nurse, factory worker, doctor, coal miner, teacher, or lawyer, their experiences, how much they loved (or hated) their job, likely influenced your choices as well.

Not all learned behaviors are positive.

We have seen cycles of endless poverty around the world. People who grew up not knowing if they were going to have breakfast, lunch, or dinner that day, making the same choices, either through addiction, lack of ambition, or just accepting their fate in life, choosing the same path, which results in generational poverty.

If you grew up in a house full of alcoholics, you did one of two things. You became one yourself because that's the example that was set, or you turned against alcohol, became a nondrinker, and chose a different kind of life.

The key here is that not all learned behaviors need to be repeated, but many of the behaviors we see influence us, the choices we make, and the lives we choose to lead.

Early in the pandemic, I was sitting in my office going through emails and checking the messages from my team from the previous day. The time was around 5:15 a.m.

My text messaging service for my business, which is connected to my email went off, so I jumped in there to see who the heck was texting me so early in the morning.

It was a doctor from the great state of Oklahoma, where it was 4:15 a.m. He sent me a note, inquiring about resume services and wanted to know if he could set up a call with my team.

Instead of texting back and forth, I asked him if he could talk by phone right then. He agreed. So, there we were, two strangers, chatting about the pandemic, life, new jobs, and resumes services before the sun came up.

I could immediately hear the pain in his voice and asked him, "What is going on? Why are you texting a resume service at 4 in the morning?"

So, he told me. He was an ER doctor in a rural hospital in Oklahoma. He was up, getting ready for work, and thought to himself, "I don't know if I can do this for another day."

It was very early in the Covid pandemic when there were no cures, no vaccines, no treatments to be had. Hospitals all over the world were overwhelmed with patients and there was very little they could do for them.

His hospital had admitted 35 people the day before from a local nursing home where the virus had spread like wildfire. Several people died, gasping for breath as they laid on gurneys lined up in the hallways of the ER, before they could even be seen.

He was terrified for his family, his kids, his staff, and himself. Working around the clock to save lives with no resources, no support, and no equipment. They had two respirators and there were only four beds in the ER. He said they were duct taping medical gowns around their arms and making makeshift masks and praying that no one on the staff got sick.

In all of his years as a doctor, 20 to be exact, he'd had no training or warning for how to deal with such an emergency. Rural hospitals had very little in the way of resources during normal times, but this was something they couldn't have dreamed up.

And he wanted out.

So, I set up an appointment with my team and we created an entire package for him.

Last I heard from him, he never used his new resume. After our conversation, where he told me that his dad had been a doctor and his grandfather a doctor before him, he admitted he loved being a doctor.

He felt like a coward even thinking about leaving. His whole life he saw his dad and grandpa make sacrifices, work hard, dedicate their lives in the service of others, and again, my friends, learned behavior.

But at that moment, what he wanted was an escape, or the possibility of an escape.

He loved being a doctor and was very good at it. He loved working in a rural town, he loved the small town feel of being able to spend time with patients, getting to know them and their families, and seeing them through births, deaths, and everything in between.

He later told me that once he had his resume, he felt empowered by the potential to make a change, and for him, that is what sustained him.

Eventually, supplies began to trickle in, lives were saved, the dead were buried, and he got through it. And sometimes, when we are faced with unspeakable challenges, that is all we can do.

Life lessons can be found in the strangest places. Make sure you are paying attention when one comes your way.

9

I Cannot Control
the Weather

I cannot control the weather; neither can you. We spend so much time worrying about things we cannot control. Anxiety levels and depression have skyrocketed in recent years. Mental health is a topic that has become so mainstream, most people are out there talking about their issues, situations, things that scare them, problems they have, and how they feel about it so much that it has become the proverbial watercooler conversation.

And I think that is a good thing.

I did not plan on writing a chapter about mental health in this book, but in my company, it is a topic we chat about regularly. I don't want to give you the wrong impression. I am not running around all day asking my team if they are depressed. But, if I see someone who is normally pretty happy and bubbly having an off day, I will ask, "Is everything okay?"

Sometimes they respond that they are perfectly fine. Sometimes the problem spills out of them like a rainspout. I listen. They talk. I can provide advice or guidance or support, but I am not a therapist. My advice tends to be motherly, and sometime that does the trick.

Everyone needs someone to listen to them. Whether it is at home or at work or at school, the best thing we can do as friends, employers, and peers is to listen.

I personally had terrible anxiety in my twenties and thirties, and that was a time when the world did not seem to be falling apart.

In this day and age, as the world has turned into a dumpster fire of crap, I have no anxiety at all. Maybe I grew out of it, or most likely, I began to realize as I got older that I can only control what goes on in my own life, my own family, and my own situation. Anything that causes me to worry now is probably something I've created on my own.

So, where do you find the balance?

Well, I think you start off by recognizing if you need professional help. And if you do, don't be ashamed to get it. Realizing that some worry and anxiety is normal is important. And don't feel like there is something wrong with you, there isn't.

Everyone worries. I think it gets worse when you have kids. You worry about them. A lot. Both of my kids have anxiety. One is on medication for it, one is not. But the ONE thing that works when either of them has it bad is breathing exercises.

I went to a therapist for my anxiety, and she told me that if you breathe in and out, seven times in a row, your racing heart will slow down. And that worked for me and works for my kids, who now are adults.

I remember when my own daughter had panic attacks, we would hold hands, look each other in the eye and do the seven times breathing thing. It always, always worked. I was always so proud of that, as if I invented it myself.

Here are some other things that I've found to be effective (I have had a lot of therapy, so let me share my takeaways with you).

Regular Exercise: I hate exercise. Despise it. I know that's not a popular stance when everyone is out there getting fit and looking like bikini models, so I won't tell you to exercise. But I will tell you to clean out a drawer, bake a cake, or go for a walk. The act of exercise doesn't have to be traditional exercise, it can be any activity that gets you off the couch. It could be shopping or washing your car, or my personal favorite: cleaning out a closet, dumping all the stuff I don't wear into bags, and driving them to a donation center.

Coffee and Booze: I don't drink at all. I would like to; it seems like fun. But I have one glass of wine and need to immediately go take a nap. Now, my husband, who is very quiet and shy, is the best drinker I've ever met. The more beer he drinks, the funnier he gets. He is a super witty and smart guy, but add a bit of booze, he's like a standup comedian.

There are times I've had to pop a few Advil because he makes me laugh so long and so much that my sides hurt. But drink too much and that hangover feeling, that sluggishness, THAT headache, though, can cause issues.

I had a friend whose husband would drink so much playing golf with his buddies on Saturdays, that by Sunday morning, his anxiety levels would go through the roof. She spent many Sundays at the ER with him. Of course, he thought he was having a heart attack. He was not. After a few years, she told him, "If this is what you are going to do to yourself and then expect me to spend my Sunday afternoons in the ER with you, think again. Next time, call your mother."

Coffee is a crutch that I personally struggle with. Starting off with a pot in the morning, that leads to another pot in the afternoon, and by 2 p.m., my hands are shaking, and my brain is scrambled. I love the smell, the taste, the buzz that I get from the "juice." Since I don't drink alcohol, I always thought this "lesser of two evils" approach was pretty justifiable. It's not. No human should be drinking two pots of coffee a day. Now, I switch between decaf and regular, and I have found that my brain is still functioning, I get the same satisfaction from the taste and smell, and I can button a button on my shirt without shaky hands.

So, what is the lesson? Like my grandfather would say, "Everything in moderation."

Limit News and Social Media: I have stopped watching the news. I used to jump back and forth between networks to see what was going on. I wanted to be informed. But what happens when all the news is BAD news? Nothing you can do about it. It just caused me more issues. So, now instead of worrying if my kid is riding his bike without his helmet, and imaging all the ways he can hurt him-self, I am NOW worried about wars, kidnappings, murders, the U.S. border, and who in the British Royal Family has made a fool of themselves. So, unless someone from Buckingham Palace wants to invite me to give them some advice, I have no control over them. I glance through the online newspaper from time to time, but other than that, I try to keep it to a minimum. Same with social media. I have found the more I scroll, the more restless I become. Read a book. Go for a walk on the beach or in the park. Watch a fun movie. I promise, after watching a few Disney features, which I do on a regu-lar basis, your outlook changes.

Forgive yourself. Be kind to YOU: We are not perfect. Trying to be is an exhausting and fruitless exercise. It is okay to be quirky, weird, different. We are all so busy trying to keep up with everything we see and what everyone else is doing that we forget that 99% of us just live normal lives. I am going to be 55 years old this year. I've never been to Europe. I am going to get there one of these days, but scrolling on social media and seeing everyone's extravagant, sun-filled, fun-filled European vacations was making me feel bad about this "failure." So, instead, I talk about trave-ling with my daughter, where we would go, what we would do, how many planes we would need to get there. And you know what? I think talking about it is nearly as fun as doing it. Learn to enjoy the simple pleasures and let yourself relax a bit. Everything is going to be okay.

> Never be ashamed to focus on your mental health. You and your brain have to live together your entire life. Just as you feed your body with the right fuel and food, feed your brain with the right information, content, and people.

10 | I'm a Fraud; You're a Fraud

I hate the term *imposter syndrome*. I know it is one of those fancy schmancy terms that people use to talk about stuff they don't want to talk about, but here is the deal, at one time or another in your life, you are going to get lucky. You'll get a job that you aren't qualified for. Land a deal you didn't think you had the balls to close. Land a boyfriend/girlfriend/spouse who is way above your paygrade or land a pair of $500 shoes at the thrift store, unworn, with a designer label for $10.

The textbook definition of *imposter syndrome* is a psychological pattern in which an individual doubts their accomplishments, skills, or talents and has a persistent internalized fear of being exposed as a "fraud" despite evidence to the contrary. People experiencing imposter syndrome often feel that their achievements are the result of luck or external factors, rather than their own abilities. This can lead to feelings of inadequacy, self-doubt, anxiety, and a constant fear of being "found out" by others.

I am no psychiatrist and cannot even begin to explore why people feel this way, but it is more common than you think.

While we would like to believe that all the people we look up to, admire, and hope to emulate are in jobs or positions because they are so smart, so brilliant, so driven, so capable because they are akin to business superheroes, it's just not true.

Most of us have had a lucky break from time to time, and a lot of the people you admire, while they may be smart, famous, or successful, probably didn't get there entirely on their own.

Let's deep dive into politics for a moment. Have you ever seen or heard a politician speak and think to yourself, "This person is a blathering idiot?" Or how did this person get here? They cannot string two sentences together, or I cannot believe a group of voters collectively thought this person was the best for the job. Yep, been there. But, here we are. We have elected people to roles to make decisions for our country or state who cannot tie their shoes without assistance. They probably never once think they don't deserve to be there. No imposter syndrome at all.

Yet, every day people are often mired in self-doubt, questioning their abilities to do their jobs, or worried that once they've reached the top, someone is going to come and knock them down. They are consumed by negative thoughts, worried about someone "finding out" that they are not as qualified or capable as they appear and worry their entire lives about being found out.

I am here to tell you that this is so incredibly common, so prevalent, and if you feel this way, you are not alone at all.

So what should you do to overcome it?

The first step is to acknowledge that you are experiencing imposter syndrome. Recognize that these feelings are common and that many successful people have gone through similar struggles.

Share your feelings with someone you trust—a friend, family member, mentor, or therapist. Opening up about your feelings can help alleviate the isolation and provide a different perspective on your achievements.

Make a list of your accomplishments, skills, and experiences. Reviewing your achievements can help you gain a more realistic perspective on your capabilities and remind you of your strengths. Looking at things on paper can bring clarity to your accomplishments, much like taking a list to the grocery store can help you come home with food you can actually eat for dinner, instead of Doritos and donuts, which is what I do when I go to the store. As soon as I hit the bakery, I am all of a sudden unable to remember the ingredients for the salads I was going to make for dinner, and instead, think it is a much better idea to eat cake and cookies. Don't do that. Write it down.

Encourage positive feedback from others. We have our resume clients get a few letters of recommendation or nice quotes from people they've worked with. Having someone say something nice about you, while a simple exercise, can be the words and sentiments that help you cement the idea of "Hey, I am pretty good at my job!"

Stop trying to be perfect all the time. We are a society obsessed with perfection. Size 2 dresses, perfect skin, perfect hair, picture-perfect lives. That is not attainable. It's not realistic, nor should it be. Even your favorite social media stars have bad days, get zits, can't fit into their jeans, and sometimes, their yachts break down.

Enjoy your wins. Got a raise? Celebrate it. You deserve it. Be honest with yourself and recognize the effort, dedication, and skills that contributed to your accomplishments.

And be kind to yourself. Treat yourself with the same kindness and understanding that you would offer to a friend or a peer.

I have a client who worked as a marketing assistant in a very well-known advertising agency in Chicago. She was amazing, smart, ambitious, innovative, and super creative, but she kept getting passed over for promotions she applied for. Why?

Every time she got an interview for a higher-level job, she kept talking like an admin. She could not get past how she would help "coordinate" events for clients, how she created reports to track budgets and expenditures, and how she "assisted and supported" the teams to win new business. She kept referring to herself as someone who was not in charge of anything, when, in fact, she was the reason, in many cases, why events were so successful, and why the business development team was so prepared to go into client meetings and win their business.

After several years in the same role, she came to us for resume services, and we created a narrative around why she should be in a management role. We talked about how she coached, mentored, and helped new staff to be successful. We talked about how she innovated new processes that automated client project milestones, and all kinds of other cool things she did that required a much higher level of expertise in marketing. She no longer looked, sounded, or talked like an assistant, and within a few months, she landed a marketing manager role. She was now in charge of a small team, had three major accounts that were valued over $1 million in sales, and moved from making $65,000 a year to $100,000 a year.

When she got the offer, she called me. And then promptly burst into tears. She was excited and terrified all at once. She said there was no possible way she could lead people or be in charge. I told her she was already doing these things and she absolutely could. "And besides," I said, "what's the worst thing that could happen?" I told her to "fake it 'til you make it" and just continue to do and be all the things that we both knew she can do. That was about 10 years ago.

She came to us a few years ago to get her resume updated for a chief marketing officer position for a tech startup. She got the job. Once she got over thinking about all the things she couldn't do, and started actually DOING all the things she could, that is who she became.

Another client we worked with was running information technology for a large school district. They had 11 school buildings and thousands of students, teachers, and staff. He'd been there about 11 years. He was making $125,000 and stayed in the job because his son, a special needs kiddo with autism and ADHD, was a student in that district. He wanted to be available for his son, keep an eye on his education, and make sure that the teachers knew him and that he was involved.

Despite the fact that he'd come from a much bigger IT background, was severely underpaid, and knew that his career could stall, he stayed on because he wanted to be where his kid was.

As they do, the years flew by, and pretty soon his son was a senior in high school. So, it was time for Dad to get a new position.

Here's the thing. While he was titled as an IT Manager, he was really a Chief Technology Officer at heart. He took an entire IT infrastructure from zero to hero over his time in the school district. Working with very little money, very little resources, and a small staff, he built a robust infrastructure for the district, invested in the right products, and when the pandemic hit, he moved teachers and students to a remote system within two weeks. He was smart. Solid. Accomplished. And that is how we treated his resume.

He was a bit shocked (and excited) when he got his resume draft and we had "Chief Technology Officer Candidate" splashed across the top of it. His immediate feedback was, "Hey, I am not a CTO," which is classic imposter syndrome behavior.

But I asked him to tell me all the ways he was NOT a CTO. He managed people, managed budgets, made tech buying decisions, drove strategy, kept up with the latest and greatest tools for teachers and students, fixed things that were broken, and built all the capabilities the district needed without a lot of fanfare.

He was a CTO in every way except the title. And when he started applying for jobs, employers agreed. He ended up taking a CTO role with a smallish manufacturing company and once that CTO title was on his resume, with a CTO job behind it, that was his new "professional identity."

I tell everyone this . . . if you wish to move into the executive stratosphere, try to get a job with the highest-level title that makes sense. I don't care if that company makes $1 in profit. Once you have that title on your resume, that is now who you are.

So don't be afraid of getting a VP, Director, or C-suite title in your next job. What you don't know, you'll learn. What you can't do, you'll do, and what you are scared of will eventually wither away and one day you will wake up and say, I got this.

> Never be afraid to know your value, in dollars and cents. Professionals who know what they are worth, what others are paid, and when to move on to a job that pays more, ultimately find themselves in positions where they are paid fairly.

11 | The Power of a Really, Really, Really Great Resume

In a world bustling with hopes and dreams, wherever people seek their happiness, fulfillment, paycheck, and place in the sun, the often-underestimated document known as a resume can wield an extraordinary power.

I am often quite surprised by the terrible resumes that people send over to us as they begin working with us on the process of crafting their professional stories.

Really bad layouts, generic descriptions, no pizazz or accomplishments, looking like something that was thrown together as an afterthought, I often say, "Do you realize this is the ONE thing that YOU have the power over to make an impression on a hiring manager for a job that may change your life?"

People often respond, "Well, when you put it like that, yes, this sucks!"

A well-crafted resume is more than just a piece of paper or a digital file, it is the two-page presentation of your life's work, the key that unlocks doors to opportunities, connecting professional dreams to reality. This is the story of how a seemingly unassuming compilation of experiences, skills, and aspirations has the potential to change lives.

A young man of 22 took a job at a local warehouse as an assistant shift supervisor. He has a degree in business and dreams of becoming a CEO. Smart, ambitious, and thoughtful, he jumped with both feet into the role, and soon found himself tasked with many things not originally found in his job description.

The warehouse had a very high turnover rate, staff always being hired, staff always quitting because the work was dirty, hard, and demanding.

He was making around $20 an hour.

Within two years, he had created a new training program to address not only the demands of the warehouse jobs, but also some safety concerns that had been overlooked, and a few team-boosting activities like pizza parties for the night shift, and part-time roles for college students that they'd never offered before.

So, they promoted him into a supervisor role. Now he was making $30 an hour.

A few more years go by, he has reduced the company's turnover rate by 50%; simplified its hiring processes; built a great, productive, and engaged team and there is nowhere else for him to go. He gets a few small raises, tops out at $36 an hour, which translates into about $75,000 a year.

The company can see that he has potential; it has an operations manager position at this location, but someone is already in it. So, he bides his time, waiting for a role to open up, and another year goes by. He realizes he's punching above his paygrade and knows he can do more, make more, be more.

He comes to us for resume services, and we sit and talk with him about his history. The only job he has ever had is in this warehouse, outside of some jobs while in college. We list 22 different accomplishments, include every metric that we can dig up, and he starts applying to operations manager roles in warehousing. Before long, he's landing interviews, landing offers. The one he takes starts out at $120,000. That is a $45,000 raise for those of you who cannot do math.

When someone says to one of our salespeople that they don't want to "spend the money" on a good resume, I think of that story. We put this kid in a basic package, which cost him $589 and he got a $45,000 raise and a path to being a CEO someday. That's a pretty good return on investment.

We worked with a young healthcare professional a few years back. A registered nurse (RN), with a passion for patient quality, innovation, and growth, he exited hands-on nursing to take an administrative management role in the healthcare industry.

In 2015, he accepted a $50,000 position, with the idea that he could really make a difference, contribute ideas (since he'd come from hands-on nursing), and grow with the company.

It was quickly apparent that he was not being utilized how he should have been. Every idea he suggested, every change he wanted to implement, was met with resistance. They just wanted him to be a cog in the wheel with no appreciation for his managed care background.

He decided to move into a sales role in the medical device field, where he made more money, but the company didn't really want to innovate. They kept changing his goals, resetting the sales targets, and when he exceeded 200% to plan in his territory, he was informed that he needed to work even harder.

They actually said, "this is a great opportunity for you," and didn't think he would leave just because he was young and making a lot of money.

He did leave.

In 2022, he accepted a position with a top-10 medical device company with a $300,000 salary.

He went from $50,000 to $300,000 in six years. His resume package cost him $689.

So, how did we did it? We leveraged his hands-on patient experience, with his knowledge of the managed care environment, along with his proven sales ability to make him look like the perfect fit for this job. Nurses know an awful lot about how things work. Things like insurance reimbursements, patient education, and how to successfully work with physicians, and gain their trust and their buy-in. Most sales people don't speak "medical" language coming in the door, but he did because he was a nurse. You have to use what you have, leverage it where you can, and that's exactly how we created his resume.

The new company supports his creative mind. They are using his background as an RN to innovate changes in product development, which really has a positive impact on quality and patient outcomes.

We worked with a female marketing executive who was employed at a mid-sized software company. Her actual title was marketing associate, but I say she was a marketing executive because she was doing all the things executives do.

Although her title was marketing associate, she was setting strategy, hiring and managing teams, managing a budget, and overseeing all facets of marketing, including public relations, social media, branding, website overhauls, advertising, and lead generation. She helped the company grow from $7 million to $12 million in revenue during the seven years she was there.

She kept going to company management and saying, "You need to give me a 'bigger title,'" and instead, they just kept giving her 3% and 4% yearly raises.

Marketing leaders in that size of a company make around $125,000. She was making $80,000.

When she came to us for services, she was disillusioned, depressed, and exhausted. She was giving it her all, but management was not giving her ITS all. Management just kept her at the same level, and as the company grew, she just kept getting more and more work.

Once we heard her story, her successes, we were able to package her into a marketing leader on her resume, and it resonated because, within a few months, she was offered a marketing manager role. A few years later, she landed a marketing director role, and most recently, we did an update for her and she is now the Chief Marketing Officer for a $100 million company.

It all started with a resume that focused on her actual job, instead of her job title.

Many companies will "under title" their staff to keep their pay in line with what they want or can afford to pay them, but that does not define you or your potential. It is incredibly important to know when you are performing higher-level work, but have a lower-level title.

For instance, I hate the title "Team Lead." That is a title used in a lot of retail settings, and it basically means that you are sort of the smartest or most experienced person on that team, but you are not actually in charge of anyone.

That title has made its way into mainstream companies, and now I am seeing "Team Lead" or "Project Lead" all over people's resumes. What does that actually mean?

Well, it means that you are at the top of the food chain, held responsible for the performance of yourself and others, without any of the actual perks of being a manager, that is, salaried, bonus-based compensation or the authority to make hiring, firing, or leadership decisions.

So, you are basically managing, without the management title or the commensurate management salary.

Don't fall for it. If someone offers you a job or asks you to be a "Lead" anything, find out how much more they are going to pay you, and don't be surprised when the answer is "nothing."

Almost everyone is underselling themselves on their resumes. Don't be afraid to show ALL that you do, all the ways you've contributed, and all the ways you and your employer measure your successes. While humility is a great virtue to have, there is no place for humble pie on your resume.

> Everyone, and I mean EVERYONE, has a story. Do you know how to tell yours?

12 | Famous Clients and Other People I Cannot Name

I grew up in the sticks. A very, very small town in rural Pennsylvania with a population of about 600 people. I did not encounter famous people.

Ever. No one did.

I read *Teen Beat* magazine, *People*, and later *Cosmopolitan* and *Vogue*, and could only dream about the glamourous people I saw on those pages and fantasize about the glamorous lives they led.

Which probably did not include going to church on Sunday and getting chased around the yard by my sister holding a hose while I was trying to get my tan on. Or getting one new pair of sneakers every year before the start of the school year.

We went to the movies, didn't watch them on television (highlight of the year). And the closest thing we ever experienced to fame was when the local newspaper photographer snapped a picture of my sister, who was 8 at the time, eating a giant piece of watermelon at the church fair.

That picture, with watermelon juice running down her chin as she was dressed as an Italian immigrant for the annual parade, was the source of many fits of giggles as my mom would bring it out from time to time so we could bask in the glow of her fame.

So, meeting someone famous would probably have put us in a state of stupefaction not seen since we all spent our hard-earned allowance on a pet rock. (Kids, ask your parents about this.)

So, when I started meeting people and writing their resumes, I never thought I would encounter anyone famous. Keep in mind, that 100% of our clients over the past 23 years have all been by phone/email/chat/text, and I have never met any one of them in person.

To do my job, I had to be good on the phone. And I learned how to be. It is much easier now that we live in a virtual world, but back in the early 1990s, it wasn't so common NOT to meet someone in person.

At times, I had to turn down business for people who insisted we meet at a coffee shop, or office, and had to gain their trust for my abilities all by phone.

And I did. I would chat with them about their lives, their jobs, their successes, their failures, their kids, their paychecks, their hobbies. To this day, I still have resume clients who ask about my kids by name, and I know their kids' names too. I have talked to hundreds of thousands of regular people, from all around the world, and they've shared their stories with me. For which, I am eternally grateful.

But nothing prepares you for getting a phone call from someone "famous."

The first time it happened, I was sure I was being pranked.

He explained to me that he was a personal assistant to one of Hollywood's most famous actresses. And let me tell you, it was a doozy. I cannot name her, or him, but when I tell you that this personal assistant had some juicy stories, I am not pulling your leg.

She was friends with the likes of Madonna, Michael Jackson, Marlon Brando, and had even been chummy with Marilyn Monroe back in the day. She was a much older actress, and while her acting career had been over for a long time, her fame was not.

I asked him why he needed a resume, and he told me that after 18 years as her assistant, it was time for him to move on and do something different.

Since she was no longer active on the Hollywood scene, there was not much work for him anymore, and his position had been relegated to hanging out with her for dinner, taking her dogs for walks, and helping her pack up her extensive wardrobe to be donated to charity.

While he loved her, he was still a fairly young man and wanted to travel the world, rub elbows with the beautiful people, and feel relevant again.

So, we did his resume. Normally, I spend about an hour on the phone with a client (or at least I did when that was still part of my job), but I think we probably talked for three hours or so. I told him right up front that I was completely starstruck, that I would never share his name or information with anyone, and to this day, I have not, but I was so curious, so excited, so enamored with his stories, that I could not get enough.

He told me about how she'd send private jets on a whim to bring a friend over for the weekend.

Or how she'd ask him to put together last-minute dinner parties, and he'd end up sitting next to some of the most famous musicians in the world over lobster bisque and truffle croquettes.

Or when she would decide she wanted to go shopping, in Paris, and he'd have to wake up the pilots to gas up the jet so she could be the first person in line at the Chanel Store on the Avenue des Champs-Élysées the next morning before the paparazzi would hound her or take pictures that she did not want taken.

For a country girl, it all sounded incredibly exciting!

So, he was the first in a long line of people who I would consider "famous" or "nearly famous." But there were others....

It could be a politician from a foreign country or a beleaguered executive who was making the news for all the wrong reasons. Former child actors, former musicians, former professional athletes, or people famous, or infamous, for one reason or another.

Every week, I see a client of ours on the news: CNN, FOX, MSNBC, or other networks. Someone shows up to do a segment on gun control, women's rights, the economy, healthcare, or sports, and I will say to my husband, "We did his/her resume."

It always makes me feel like a proud mama. Like I had something to do with their success. Maybe I did.

I was working with an executive client in the healthcare industry in the United States. She was a phenomenal human, a really genuine person who cared about people and the quality of care they were receiving in one of the largest healthcare systems in the U.S. South. After working with her, she ended up getting an even higher-level leadership position and she was always sending people my way.

One day, she sent me a note that one of her friend's sons had just retired from the NFL. It may surprise you that many professional football players, or professional athletes from many sports, still must work once they retire from the sport. Not every professional athlete makes millions of dollars, and a lot of these kids are pretty young when they get hurt or get cut. So, they need resumes just like everyone else.

In this case, he was fairly well known, had made it about eight years in the NFL, but he was having a different kind of job challenge.

When he retired from the NFL, he invested his money in restaurants and nightclubs in his hometown of a large southern city, where he was hailed as a local hero.

So, every evening, he would spend his time surrounded by his fans, shaking hands, slapping shoulders, and generally living out his glory days with the adoration of his many, many, many (female) fans.

The problem was, he was married with three kids. And while his wife adored him, too, she was not of the mind to feed his ego, slap his shoulder, and be regaled with tales of his on-field antics.

She mostly wanted him to take out the garbage, give their kids a bath, and help put them to bed.

So, she very sweetly issued him an ultimatum (from the South, so I am sure some of her comments included things like "Bless your little heart" and "I was born at night, but not last night") and told him, "It is either us (your family) or them (your groupies). You can still be an investor, but you need to get a different job."

So, he came to us. And he was a great guy, humble and well spoken, very excited about his previous career and his future. So, we developed a resume for him, like we have done with many former professional athletes, by putting his sports career front and center on his resume.

Let's face it. Being a former professional athlete is a conversation starter. We do it with all of our famous or semi-famous clients. If you are applying for a sales job or a position in public relations or marketing, and you are a former athlete, you are almost guaranteed an interview. It is just the world we live in.

Now, trying to equate playing football or baseball or basketball with business is a story for another day, but it can be done.

We started off talking about his education (business administration), his career, his relationships, his wins, his losses, his experience mentoring younger players, and the community service he's done, and voilà, you have a resume.

Last I heard, he accepted a position as an athletic director at a private school in his area. I am sure the kids, parents, and other coaches are thrilled. So is his wife.

One day, I answered the phone and there was a gentleman who was a Chief Operating Officer for a very large international telecommunications company on the other end. It was early in the day, I had not showered, or brushed my teeth, and was in a 15-year-old threadbare nightgown chatting with this guy like I was sitting on the deck of my yacht reading *The New York Times*.

I was not. I had just put my kids on the school bus and was tackling emails like I do every morning.

He was reaching out for resume services because his company was in trouble. He was in trouble. Wall Street was all over him; the investors were screaming, revenue was down, morale was down, their R&D was in the toilet and they were losing market share like nobody's business.

So, here I was, the person he was looking to for help.

While we were chatting, I Googled him. Several years previously, he had been on the cover of *Forbes* magazine and the inside feature showed the huge California home that he and his wife had renovated.

While it would be easy to say, "Oh how the mighty have fallen," that's not my style.

He was a person, just like any other person who is reaching out for help.

A hard-working guy, faced with some tough economic shifts, a changing competitive market, and some bad decisions we've all been there, he was looking to get out. So we worked with him, and he moved on into a much less high-profile job, and lived a much happier life.

It doesn't matter if you've been the CEO, the janitor, or a world-class athlete every single person struggles in their career. You will not love every job you have. You will not have a great boss everywhere you go. You will not be fulfilled, paid what you are worth, or even treated nicely at every job. But every single one of those experiences makes up YOUR experience, and how you handle pressure, an incompetent boss, a terrible paycheck, or a job failure—it all counts toward your accumulated experiences that make up a successful career.

Navigating the job search can be a challenging and humbling experience, and it's important to remember that everyone, regardless of their previous job title or salary, can face similar struggles. Here is some advice for job seekers on how to handle these challenges:

Stay Resilient: Understand that rejection and setbacks are a natural part of the job search process. Everyone faces them, no matter their background. Stay resilient, keep a positive attitude, and remember that each rejection brings you closer to the right opportunity.

Networking: Networking is a powerful tool in the job search, and it's something everyone can do, regardless of their previous position. Reach out to former colleagues, friends, and acquaintances. Attend networking events and engage with professionals in your field to expand your circle.

Skills and Self-Improvement: Focus on continuous self-improvement and skill development. Enhance your resume and qualifications by taking courses, certifications, or gaining new experiences. Your willingness to learn and adapt is a valuable asset.

Adaptability: Be open to a wide range of opportunities. Sometimes, a change in job title or industry can lead to a fulfilling career. Be adaptable and consider how your skills can transfer to different roles. No one ends up where they start out. Be open to all kinds of opportunities, and just because you were once a teacher, doesn't mean you have to be a teacher forever. People move successfully back and forth between industries all the time. So, don't pigeonhole yourself into one thing or another.

Professional Branding: Invest time in your online presence, including your LinkedIn profile and resume. Make sure your resume is telling a great story, that your LinkedIn profile is genuine and approachable.

Persistence: The job search process can be a long and arduous journey. Keep in mind that finding the right opportunity often takes time. Stay persistent, maintain a consistent job search routine, and don't get discouraged by temporary setbacks. Some people will find a new job in two weeks, others it can take five or six months. Take any interviews you are offered, make connections anywhere you interview and in the future, even if you don't get a job there now, you can always reach back out when a company has something posted that is of interest to you.

Stay Positive: Maintain a positive mindset and remember that no one opportunity defines you, that everyone gets rejected from a job, and that your job search is an opportunity to develop resilience. I once had a client who applied to 74 different roles within a huge commercial construction company before he got one interview. He had always wanted to work for them, and every single job he saw that was a fit, he sent his resume. It took six months, but he finally got the call and got the offer.

> No matter who you are, what you do, how much money you make, or how successful you become, nothing lasts forever, and sometimes, it is just time to move on.

13

There Are All Kinds of Jobs

In the United States, there are thousands upon thousands of job titles. There are also many, many types of job classifications.

Most of us think of a job as a 9 to 5, Monday through Friday type of situation, but in fact, there is more than one way to earn a living.

The U.S. Bureau of Labor Statistics categorizes over 800 occupations or types of occupations. They include the following:

- Management
- Business and financial operations
- Computer and mathematical
- Architecture and engineering
- Life, physical, and social science
- Community and social service
- Legal
- Educational
- Library
- Arts
- Design

- Entertainment
- Sports
- Media
- Healthcare
- Technical
- Building and grounds cleaning and maintenance
- Farming
- Fishing
- Forestry

. . . and the list goes on and on and on.

If you took a "what do I want to be when I grow up" test in high school or college, it seems like it was a much narrower window. Most of the test results included things like teacher, accountant, nurse, scientist, librarian, or customer service representative. Or my personal favorite: marine biologist. I saw marine biologist on every single test I took. I grew up thinking there were way more opportunities to be a marine biologist than there actually are.

Just a funny little story about marine biologists. As I was finishing this book, my daughter and I took the ferry from New Jersey into New York City for the famous San Gennaro Festival in Little Italy. It was a beautiful sunny day, and we enjoyed our time on the ferry just as much as our time in the city. As we were headed back to Jersey, we met two brothers who were also headed home. We chatted, talked about the city, and what a beautiful day it was. One of the young men told me he had been traveling for several weeks up and down the East coast doing research on water quality and pollution. "Wow, how interesting," I said. "What do you do for a living?" He answered, "I am a marine biologist." His name was Liam, and he is part of an extraordinary organization called New Logic Marine Science Camp. If you love the water and the beach as much as I do, check them out. They are doing great work teaching kids how to care and preserve our oceans!

Then, if you throw in occupational categories like:

- unskilled/semi-skilled/skilled labor
- professional/managerial positions

- full time/part time/temporary/permanent/gig positions
- union/non-union jobs

. . . the opportunities are simply endless.

So why do most of us grow up thinking we can only be in sales or management or human resources or healthcare?

Is it because of what we see and hear around us?

Most farmers make a pretty good living. But how many farmers do you actually know? Unless you were born into farming, or you've had some kind of crazy midlife crisis and buy a goat farm, you've probably never thought of being a farmer.

We've been watching television shows in which police officers, detectives, doctors, and lawyers rule the day and everything we see, hear, listen to, and watch on social media influences our decisions.

In my generation, we viewed doctors and lawyers as the most successful professions. They were always dressed in suits or scrubs, drove nice cars, and lived in nice houses. But younger generations think they can make a living on social media by being influencers or by selling pictures of their feet on the internet. Yes, the world can be a strange place.

When we interview clients for their resumes, we always ask "What do you want to be when you grow up?" Of course, most of our clients are already well past the age of starting their careers, but this question is a good ice breaker, generates a laugh, and gets people talking about their goals. Most of the time, they name a title they are after, a promotion they want, or an industry they'd like to work in.

Then, we delve a bit deeper. Asking things like: "Do you like managing others?" Or: "What did you like most about your last job?" Or: "Tell me about the job you've had that you consider to be your favorite, and why?" Once we get those answers, we can begin to see what environment they like, and which responsibilities get them excited about going to work.

So, those are the things you should ask yourself when determining where you would like to go next in your career. If you are someone who dislikes being responsible for others, you should probably not be applying for management or leadership roles. If you are outgoing, love landing deals, and get excited by the prospect of winning new customers, then you should be looking at sales or business development roles.

People don't really think about their careers that way. A lot of times, they say "I will take whatever, as long as the pay is decent and I get the weekends off."

The average human being will spend 97,760 hours working in their lifetime. That is a lot of hours. If you run it all together, you spend about as much time working as you do sleeping in your lifetime. You will probably spend as much time working as you do with your family. Or more.

Like the old saying goes, "When you do something you love, you will never spend a day working in your life." So, how do you answer the age-old question: "How to find a job you love?"

Finding a job you love can be a fulfilling and rewarding experience, but it often requires time, self-reflection, and proactive effort. Here are some actions to help you find a job you love:

- While most careers tend to be "fly-by-the-seat-of-your-pants" affairs, the successful job seekers will do some self-assessment that includes:
  - Reflect on your interests, passions, and values. What activities make you feel happiest and most fulfilled?
  - Identify your strengths and weaknesses as well as the skills you excel in and enjoy using.
  - Consider your long-term goals and what you want to achieve in your career and life.
- Do your research. Explore different industries, job roles, and companies that align with your interests and values. Look beyond the surface to understand the day-to-day responsibilities and work culture.
- Network with professionals in your desired field to gain insights and learn about their experiences. Find a mentor. That can be someone in your personal or professional circle.
- Set some goals. Be realistic. If you are a recent college graduate, you are not going to get called for a vice-president–level

job. Assess your actual skills. Good with people? Love high-energy work environments? Have a passion for sports, fitness, food, clothes, jewelry, cars, or video games? Look at entry level positions in those industries and see where you would be a good fit. Then customize your resume with relevant keywords and apply!

■ If you are a more mature candidate and are ready to move into a director-level role, set the goal. Set the timeline and work toward it. Meet with your boss and let them know of your ambitions, and work together to create a plan of action to grow your responsibilities and talents to achieve that title in your desired timeline. When you get your current employer on board and can get your boss on your side, career growth can be fostered from within. If you are met with disdain, no assistance, no help, or no support, it may be time to look elsewhere.

■ Invest in acquiring the necessary skills and knowledge for your desired job or industry. This might involve taking courses, attending workshops, or earning certifications.

■ Continuously improve your existing skills and stay up-to-date with industry trends.

■ Sometimes the best thing you can do for your career is meet people who are already where YOU want to be. Attend industry events, conferences, and seminars to meet professionals in your field.

■ Leverage social media platforms to connect with like-minded individuals and potential mentors.

Finding the perfect job might take time. Some people spend years finding it. Don't give up, take all opportunities that come your way. Think outside of the norm when you are looking for jobs.

Many, many professionals are what I call "accidentally successful." They took a chance in a position that may not have been that perfect fit, but found a home with a company they love, in a role they excel in, and were able to use that as a steppingstone to get a job they truly love.

My husband and I were sitting at the end of a long deck at a restaurant called The Proving Ground in Atlantic Highlands, New Jersey.

The restaurant is on the ocean, and boats can come there to dock. Its passengers disembark and head into the restaurant to enjoy lunch, dinner, or cocktails. The food is fantastic, they have live music, and it is a popular joint. There is a long deck filled with rocking chairs where you can relax, enjoy the ocean views, and have a few cocktails of your own.

One such sunny summer day, we headed there to grab some lunch. We had a 90-minute wait for our table, so we retired to the rocking chairs to pass the time. As passengers get off the boats, everything from small sailboats to million-dollar yachts, they come through a gate that just so happens to be exactly where we were sitting.

I felt like a greeter! More than 50 people disembarked during the time we sat there, and I chatted with every single one of them. Yes, it is a rare talent, but I digress.

So, we were watching the deck master handling the influx of boat traffic, and he was telling people where to dock, escorting folks off the boats, tying the boats to the dock, and generally being a boat traffic cop. At one point, there were too many boats trying to dock, and he would instruct them to head out about 500 yards and drop anchor. He would then retrieve the parties and bring them to the deck.

During a lull, we started chatting with him. A very interesting guy, dressed in boat shoes, countless tattoos, a deep tan, and healthy head of long hair, which he had tied back in a ponytail.

He told us he'd been working there for many years, loves the water, and works year-round. He regaled us with tales of drunken passengers, people who get seasick and never get back on the boat, and how most days, he starts at 10 a.m. and works late into the evenings when the last reservations return to their boats.

I cannot tell you how many times I have thought about that conversation. Why? Well, most people don't think about being a deck master at a restaurant. He seemed so happy, so relaxed, and so proficient at his work, and I would bet you a dollar that he never once said growing up, "I'd like to be a deck master at a restaurant that caters to boaters."

How so many of us end up in jobs that we never even thought about? That's how life happens, right? Some of us just float through our careers, taking one job after another until we find something we really love. Some of us have a definitive idea of what we want to be and pursue and pursue it until we get there. There is no right or wrong way to go about it.

Another guy I talked to that day was waiting with his wife for a table, just like we were. He was limping around the walkway and happened to be standing in front of us when we exchanged hellos. I asked him if he was injured, and he told me that he had just had knee replacement surgery and was having a hard time getting around.

I said to him, "You seem to be too young for a knee replacement" (keeping in mind he was around my age—mid-fifties—and I consider myself to be a spring chicken). He told me that he was a football player in college and passed up the chance to join the NFL. His family originally hailed from Italy, and he had always wanted to live there. So, he tried out for an Italian Pro Soccer League, made the team, and spent a decade playing professional soccer in Italy.

A career-ending knee injury resulted in him moving back to the United States, where he and a friend opened a landscaping business. He had knee replacement surgery in his forties, but recently had to have another one, and because of his inability to walk, bend, and do any type of manual labor, he recently sold his business. After he heals, he and his partner are going to start flipping houses. To me, this is reflective of most of our career journeys. Being able to pivot, change, adapt, and choose a new path can take us places we never thought we'd be.

That day I met a professional musician, an owner of a car dealership, a make-up artist, and a podiatrist. All jobs that most of us never think about. So as you embark, enhance, or want to change your professional direction or look for a new career, don't discount the kinds of things you never thought about. Some of the most interesting jobs are ones that you've never considered at all. One of them might be the perfect job for you.

> When you focus on making a life, instead of making a living, you often end up with the best of both worlds.

14 | New Grad? So Rad!

You've done it. You've graduated from college! Cheers to you, and your parents/family for supporting you, your hopes, your dreams, and your future career.

You've worked hard, soaked up an incredible amount of (some useless) information, learned how to live on your own (did you?), and made friends with people who are nothing like you. You are now an expert in boys/girls/beer pong/classic literature/video games/partying/how to pull an all-nighter, and pass tests that you have not studied for. Not even a little bit.

Now what? Well, your four-year (or more) quest for higher learning has come to an end, and while it was fun while it lasted, it is time to move up, move on, get a job, and live your life!

If you are one of the lucky few to have graduated college with no student loans, kudos to you. That is one less thing you have to worry about. But you will still need to learn how to "adult," get an apartment, get a job, show up on time, get along with your new peers, listen to your new boss, and not only learn something, but contribute something as well.

If you DO have student loans, keep in mind that starting those payments are going to come due before the end of the year, so factor in those monthly payments before signing an apartment lease with a hot tub, doorman, and laundry service. You probably can't afford it.

In all seriousness, college is such a fun, rewarding, and enthralling experience, and while you may have learned the basics of your major, whether its accounting or engineering or law, the hands-on experience you get in your first job is going to surpass everything you learned in four years at school, so pick wisely.

I have found that through my own experiences as a resume company owner, and a mother, that most universities are amazing at teaching you practical, philosophical, problem-solving, and applicable knowledge. They are extremely bad at teaching you how to write a resume or look for a job.

My own daughter graduated from a well-known college in New York City, and while she has a $200,000 undergraduate degree in English Lit, her professors' attempts to guide her class on preparing a resume for a modern-day job search fell embarrassingly short.

During the last days of her senior year, she attended a "Senior Seminar," during which the school provided some tips and tools on preparing your resume, how to conduct a job search, and how to answer some common interview questions.

When the professor made a suggestion on what color paper you should print your resume on, my daughter gallantly stood up, dared to disagree with 90% of what he was saying, and gave her fellow soon-to-be graduates some practical advice.

Flustered and a bit annoyed, the professor said, "Alexa, why do you think you know so much about this?" She, having lived most of her life in a bedroom right next to my home office (and listening to me talk on the phone to customers for years, and years, and years), told him, "My mother owns a resume-writing business, and I've been watching and listening to her all my life."

Needless to say, he was flabbergasted, and annoyed. He said, "I didn't even know there was such a thing 'as a professional resume business.'" So there you have it folks, a highly educated university professor woefully misinformed and ill prepared to prepare YOU for the grown up world.

I have been fortunate to work with many new graduates in my career and I am going to give you some honest and forthright guidance on how to prepare your resume and your job search for success.

First, your resume does not begin when you graduate, it begins long before then. By the time you have turned 16 or 17, you've probably had a few jobs. Whether it is babysitting, working in a fast-food restaurant, lifeguarding, or working in your parents business, you've learned a thing or two. You've picked up some skills.

There is nothing more amazing than a young lifeguard who has saved someone from drowning.

Or a fast-food worker who won "employee of the month" seven times.

Or a babysitter who has wrangled several toddlers for an entire summer, teaching them Spanish, or learning new games to keep them entertained, motivated, and engaged for 90 solid days.

Or a young volunteer, who has gone on a mission trip, traveled to a foreign country, worked at the food bank, or supervised kids at a summer camp.

All are resume-worthy experiences.

Then, how about the groups or sports you played in high school? Absolutely, add it in. Sports participation shows your ability to work as a team, and win or lose, you've successfully completed a season or competition.

If you were president of the Latin Club, like yours truly, include it. If you played football, were a cheerleader, played the drums in your high school marching band and competed for a national title, include it.

Any high school experience should be at the bottom of your resume. You can leave OFF your high school GPA and SAT scores.

At the top of your resume is where it gets fun! Showcase your collegiate academic accomplishments, which can be honors, awards, fraternity or sorority participation, sports, social clubs, and the like. If you have a GPA over 3.0, include it. If you don't, leave it off.

If you graduated summa cum laude, or cum laude, include that as well, along with any honor societies or honors programs you participated in. If you were fortunate enough to participate in a travel abroad semester, describe it, along with any language skills you picked up and experiences you had.

Now, add in any part-time, work study, or summer jobs during your four-year (or however long) college career, describe what you learned as opposed to what you did. For instance, if you were waiting tables, don't describe what a waiter is, everyone knows that. Tell me why you were a great waiter! Were you often requested by customers? Did you win recognition for your dedication to customer service? Did you learn how to make a mean Sangria? Include it.

Resumes don't and should not be boring. The more genuine reflection they are of you, the better.

Take jobs at school, try to get a work study position. They are plentiful at college and the experience is an excellent addition to your resume.

I cannot stress enough the importance of internships. In fact, I suggest to all college students that they start applying for and taking internships during their sophomore year in college. The more hands-on work experience you get during college, the better your chances of landing that job after you graduate. Keep copies of your performance feedback from your internships. Most internship opportunities will come not only with learning experiences, but positive feedback about what you learned and what you contributed.

Learn how to network. Start a LinkedIn account. Now connect with all of your friends, high school teachers, college professors, people you've met in your jobs, your social activities, and work study programs. Once you've connected with all of your friends, connect with all of your friends' parents. They are executives, business owners, employees of companies that you may want to apply to. Did you know that 46% of all referred candidates get an interview? That is MUCH better than 3% of your applications resulting in an interview. The more you can build your network, the better. These are people who see your work firsthand. They can vouch for you as recommendations, pave the way to interviews within the company when the time comes for you to start looking for a "real job."

Ask everyone to leave you a recommendation on LinkedIn or write you a letter of recommendation. Those are critical in a job application when you are nearly "unproven" as an entry level professional.

Okay, now for the social media part. Do you know how many candidates' job applications have been sunk once the company perused their social media accounts? Plenty. Who can forget the famous story of the young lady who had her offer to be the Editor-in-Chief of *Teen Vogue* rescinded once several unfortunate videos of her college days came out? You do not want to be that person.

In high school and college, follow this rule of thumb. If you are ready to post something racy, dirty, inappropriate, or, heaven forbid, illegal, ask yourself this question: "Would I be comfortable with my grandmother seeing this post?" If the answer is "no," don't post it.

Look, many of us have posted stupid things in the heat of the moment, but it is critical that you review all of your social media accounts and activities, starting around your junior year of college, and remove, delete, and destroy anything that does not present you in a positive light.

As you are looking for your first post-college job, continue learning and improving your skills. Write two or three different cover letters to accompany your resume and application. Have a little library to draw from, so that as you are applying, you are not slowing down the process by having to customize every letter.

Host an interview preparation party. Invite your fellow entry-level friends and practice common questions. See how others do it, have a few laughs, and work out your nerves.

Be courteous and professional. I know, those college graduation gift "thank you notes" are still sitting on your desk. Finish those, send them off, and when you get an interview, don't wait three months to send a thank-you letter. Always follow up after an interview, preferably within 24 hours.

Be patient. The search process can be challenging, especially for entry-level candidates. Stay patient and persistent in your efforts. If you need to, get a part-time or summer job to get some extra money to hold you over. Better yet, if you're able to, take a month or two off, enjoy your accomplishments, and start applying in August or September when the market is not flooded with new college graduates all vying for the same job.

Do something crazy. Take a job on a cruise ship, or a position in a foreign country. Take six months off and travel across the United States by van. Real life doesn't have to start right at this very minute. You are going to be working for a long time and a little adventure never hurt anyone.

Stay positive, apply for jobs outside of your comfort zone, try new things. Job searching can be challenging, but maintaining a positive attitude and staying motivated can make a big difference in your success.

> It's an exciting world out there for new graduates.

15

Criminally Insane

We have worked with hundreds of thousands of customers through the years. This story is one of my favorites.

A woman named Deb called my office for resume services. She was (and is) a nurse. I loved working with nurses to develop their resumes and grew to know so much about nursing that, after talking with a client, I could write an amazing resume in an hour.

I first start off by interviewing the client to find out about their history, what sets them apart, what sort of unique experiences they had, yada, yada, yada. And then I create their professional stories with a focus on what they want to do next.

Well, Deb had quite a unique story to tell. Over the past 15 years, she held 40 (give or take) contract roles in the nursing field. She had a 15-year career in what they call "bedside" nursing, which means she took care of patients in a hospital.

But, when the hospital she was working for started cutting back staff, she took a short-term contract job in a psychiatric hospital for children.

Her first assignment was working at an in-patient clinic with young people, mostly girls, with eating disorders that had gotten so bad that their parents had no other alternative than to admit them to a psychiatric hospital for treatment.

Deb described spoiled rich girls who threw up their steak dinners for fun (and flat bellies), and pre-teen girls whose hearts gave out because they stopped eating completely trying to attain waif-like/model-like figures. Complete with thigh gaps and protruding hip bones. Heartbreaking.

From there, Deb moved into other psychiatric settings. One such clinic held kids adopted from foreign countries who suffered from reactive detachment disorder and failure to thrive syndrome because they were never picked up or cuddled or held during their time in overcrowded orphanages. When unsuspecting U.S. parents adopted them, they did not know they were in for a lifetime of heartbreak with their new child.

The program was called "Love Is Not Enough" and it was designed to try to get these children to some sort of baseline behavior so they could co-exist in the family home.

We all remember that news story about the American mother who packed up and sent her adopted son back because she could not handle his violence, screaming, and generally unruly behavior. She sent him on a plane. By himself. Back to Russia. With a note.

While it is incredibly sad to hear these stories from Deb, it was also incredibly scary. Some of the children were prone to violent outbursts, punching, hitting, and in some cases, stabbing their nonadopted siblings or parents. Deb talked about kids being admitted to the psychiatric unit after setting fires to their family homes.

Parents locked their kids' bedroom doors using industrial locks. Locked the kids in their bedrooms with locks OUTSIDE the doors and locked up guns, knives, baseball bats, and anything that could be used as or perceived to be a weapon.

I don't know about you, but the only thing my parents ever locked up was booze and maybe a dirty magazine. I cannot imagine having to lock up the knives AND the kids at bedtime.

There were instances of families sending their biological children to live with their grandparents, while the well-intentioned adoptive parents lived in fear for their lives and had almost no resources on how to handle these kids.

That was Deb's job. To take care of the kids, help the families where she could, and do her best to make sure no one got hurt in the process. Heartbreaking without a doubt, and outcomes that were eerily similar. Very few kids went back to their families. Most of them stayed in the ward, aged out of the system, and then went to halfway houses or on the street to fend for themselves.

After that, Deb took an assignment in a prison for the criminally insane. Yep, you heard that right. There are prisons and prison wards dedicated to people found to be criminally insane. People who are so violent, so ill, so sick, so dangerous that most of them will never exist outside of their prison walls.

In this job, Deb told me she had "found her people." No, Deb is not insane. But like most good nurses, she had the right mix of empathy, no-nonsense sensibility, and a commonsense approach to helping patients. She did not judge, found no joy in troubles or sorrow of others, and she did not get emotionally involved in this setting. Every single time an inmate visited her in her office, they were chained and accompanied by an armed guard.

"This job," she told me, "was straightforward." Her goal was to keep the patients/inmates as close to their baseline as possible. With drugs. Or treatments. Or care. If they hurt themselves, she sewed them up. If they were sick, she gave them medicine. If they were dying, she held their hand while they passed. Her job was not rehabilitation.

Deb made around $35 an hour as a bedside nurse. As a contractor, she made between $85 and $100 per hour. That's why she held 40 contract assignments. She would work six months on, take six months off.

Not a bad gig if you don't mind the company you keep.

As professionals, we find "our people" all over the place. I have found that the happiest people are not necessarily the ones who make the most money. The happiest employees are the ones that enjoy their co-workers, make friends with their peers who spill into their personal lives, and get their fulfillment by the relationships they've created. Ask anyone who has been in a miserable job what made the situation bearable. Most times, it is a funny, supportive, or empathic co-worker who may be experiencing the same thing. There is no greater joy at work than great co-workers. They are the ones who not only make the daily grind more enjoyable, but also serve as a support system in your career journey. Finding your tribe in the workplace is like uncovering a treasure chest of opportunities for growth, fun, and camaraderie. Together, you overcome challenges, celebrate successes, and forge a sense of belonging in an environment that can sometimes feel overwhelming. It's a reminder that success is not solely measured by individual achievements, but by the strength and synergy of the relationships you cultivate with your fellow adventurers in the corporate world.

> Success is not a solitary pursuit, but a collective voyage, enriched by the relationships we foster along the way.

16

Looking for a Job Is Like Having a Job

In 2023, there was a gut punch heard around the world. Between economic, civil, business, and political chaos, hundreds of thousands of people lost their jobs in the United States.

Worries about a looming recession, general corporate greed, and the recognition that many, many, many companies over-hired during the pandemic ended, and now there was a fire sale of talented and smart professionals, by the thousands.

Watching business sectors collapse was like watching dominoes fall, without the same giddy excitement that we feel when the last piece falls.

The tech sector shredded workers like I shred cheese. A lot of it.

Then banking, then warehousing, then crypto, then consulting. Huge layoffs by Meta, Disney, Walmart, Lyft, Amazon, Boeing, Dell, IBM, and many, many more.

In a normal workforce environment, people leave jobs when they are unhappy, they are mistreated, when they want to make more money, or they want to move up.

But when all you hear on the news is layoff, layoff, layoff, it makes you scared to make a move.

And that is right where they want us.

During the Covid pandemic, we worked with clients in transportation, supply chain, and logistics roles who regularly took new jobs that doubled their salaries. Those functions were so desperate for leadership, they were throwing out salary dollars like drunks in a strip club.

If there was a phrase for hiring during that time, it would have been "name your price," such was the desperation of employers to hire competent (and semi-competent) people.

We were stuck in our houses, watching Netflix, and ordering stuff from Amazon like our lives depended on it, and business was booming. It was the era of the "candidate was in charge" like no other.

But in 2023, boy, did that change. Once companies realized they could not sustain or did not need all those people, the layoffs began.

So, how do you go from easily getting a job to now competing with hundreds of thousands of newly laid off people?

You dig in. You work at it every day. You write a good resume, you network, you ask your friends, families, peers, your boss from 1989, and anyone and everyone who has something nice to say about you to make introductions to jobs that their companies are hiring for.

And you accept that fact that most job searches take three months, four months, six months.

Most hiring doesn't happen fast anymore.

I talked to a client recently who is on round 17 out of an expected 20 rounds of interviews for ONE job. Yes, you read that right.

Hiring is so slow, so inept, so paralyzed, that now you have to interview someone 20 times before you make them an offer.

You've already told your very best professional story, your history, and your accomplishments on your resume and LinkedIn profile, what else can you do? The good news is there are still some things in your control.

First, keep a positive attitude. People who are negative, frustrated, short, or angry while engaged in a job search often don't find much success. People pick up on it. It's okay to be sad, angry, and hurt in private, but as you are chatting or interviewing with people, put on your happiest, most positive and most successful face.

Second, there is a famous quote by Albert Einstein, "The definition of insanity is doing the same thing over and over again, but expecting different results." This quote cannot be any truer for job seekers.

I hear from hundreds, sometimes thousands of people who say, "I've sent my resume out, or put in applications for 800, 1,000, or 2,000 jobs, and I am not getting any interviews." They think the job market is "bad."

There is almost nothing I would do on God's green earth a thousand times and get no results.

If you have been in this boat, change it up. Rewrite your resume 100 times if you need to. So many qualified people undersell themselves. Which is funny to me. We will post our lunch on social media for the world to see, but we feel "uncomfortable" bragging about our successes. Just as an FYI, this "underselling" happens more to women than men. Women are much less comfortable showcasing their leadership, operational, and career accomplishments than men.

Get over it.

Third, own your time. Keep doing things that work, like networking and applying for jobs as soon as they get posted. Eliminate time-sucking things like customizing cover letters or filling out endless applications. Applying for a job should be fairly quick. If you encounter applications that include tests, quizzes, and so on, move on. They can take hours to complete, and I've found that most of those test-type obstacles are designed to keep you out instead of letting you in.

Fourth, don't let desperation make you take a job a level or two from your career trajectory. If you are desperate, get a part-time job, do something else until the right position comes along. Most people are too proud to leave a corporate or professional role and go to wait tables, work in retail, or do things they consider "beneath them." There is nothing beneath you. There is nothing beneath me either.

It is a great way to coast along until you get the job you deserve. If you do decide to accept a position that is not in line with your salary or your level of experience, it doesn't always turn out so great. Most people start off feeling resentful and companies recognize that you are overqualified pretty quickly. That can cause problems among the dynamics in a company, and let's say your new boss has 10 less years of experience than you . . . it can be a job killer.

And finally, fifth: any company playing "hide the potato" with salary, salary ranges, benefits, compensation packages, perks, and so on, by your first or second interview, bow out. Great salaries are not a secret. In this day and age, salary transparency is key. If you don't know the salary range up front or have some idea by the first or second touch, it probably is not what you want it or wish for it to be.

> The hardest part of looking for a job is often the last step before success. Keep pushing through, for just around the corner, your next great adventure could begin.

17 | Confidence Is a Negotiation Skill

Have you ever been to a party, in a meeting, or some other social event, and someone walks into the room and immediately commands the attention of everyone in the room?

I know you've seen it in movies. I know you've seen it at work. But have you ever wondered what those people have that you don't?

The answer is probably confidence. Or otherworldly good looks. But that is a conversation for another day.

I always wanted to be the lady at the grocery store, you know the one, who is perfectly put together, coiffed hair, great outfit, freshly manicured nails, high heels, and a designer purse. She seems confident, in charge. She knows what she is there for and everyone from the kid at the deli to the gal at the pharmacy treats her with respect. But when I run to the grocery story, I am typically in day-old hair, potentially a pair of pajamas under my sweatshirt, and praying to God I don't run into anyone I know as I grab toilet paper, milk, and coffee creamer before I slink out the door.

Confidence comes from feeling good about yourself. How you look, how you dress, how you walk, talk, and capture the attention of others. The more you do it, the better you are at it, the more people relate, listen, and respect you.

Imagine being a manager, in charge of a team of people, and those people regularly come to you for advice, guidance, and direction for something they are struggling with in their jobs.

If you listen to their problems, offer support and solutions that make sense, and do it in a way that says, "I can help you or solve your problem," you've probably inspired confidence in your team. They want to do well for you. They want to make you proud. They know you have their back.

Now imagine the same scenario, but the boss is flaky, can't answer the question, gets upset at you for interrupting their work, tells you to figure it out or offers unhelpful advice. Your team is probably not too confident. In fact, you will probably get a reputation for being a jerk. Or dumb. Or both.

Now, let's talk about negotiation.

We negotiate all day long. You just don't think about it that way, but you do.

Parents negotiate with their kids to do their homework. They negotiate with their toddlers to eat their veggies. They negotiate with their co-workers to take on more work, take over a project, or assume new responsibilities to help the team.

And how do successful negotiators win? They leverage their confidence to make you feel like you made the decision yourself or presented their case so successfully that you quickly agreed to their terms.

Confidence, in the context of negotiation, doesn't imply arrogance or overbearing behavior. It is merely a firm belief in your own abilities, knowledge, and value.

Take, for instance, a marketing executive who, after 22 years with the same company, decided to apply for a chief marketing officer position. She was making over $250,000 in her job, but the CMO role paid $400,000 and she absolutely had the skills to do the work.

So, she applied, and applied some more, and started getting called into interviews.

She kept trying to bend to the will of the companies, going through endless rounds of interviews, preparing extensive marketing presentations, and for one company she spent two weeks building out a full-year marketing strategy. Which they gladly accepted, then ghosted her.

Increasingly frustrated, she kept interviewing more and more and getting nowhere.

Then, one day, she woke up and said to herself, "I am better than this." She familiarized herself with her portfolio of accomplishments, changed her attitude, and when potential employers reached out, she acted a bit aloof, asked questions about the interview processes, required that they divulge the salary up front, and (this was the hard part) she'd end the call, not committing to the interview, but saying instead "I will get back to you if I am interested."

Holy moly! The gumption! But it worked.

She shifted the perspective of being a "candidate" looking for a job, to someone they immediately wanted to chase after.

This can be hard for anyone to do, but women especially; we tend to be more "people pleasers" and want to jump at the chance to be agreeable.

Within two months, she had several CMO offers, and she went into the negotiation stage with the same kind of confidence, exuding a positive aura that set the tone for the entire process.

When she negotiated her final offer, which went from $385,000 to $425,000, she clearly laid out her body of work, her understanding of the fair market value salary for a CMO in her sector, and they agreed. This level of confidence encourages assertiveness without crossing into being too aggressive. When you stand up for yourself, know your value, and can articulate it, you will be much more successful at the negotiation table.

Salary negotiations are an intricate dance. Confidence can be the key to getting what you want. So, finding that confidence is your first step in finding the salary you want.

The ability to articulate, convince, and influence others could mean a $20,000 or $100,000 difference to your bottom line.

When you put it in numbers like that, doesn't that make you want to get a little boost of confidence for your next salary negotiation? Of course it does!

To take it a step further, you must also have the confidence to walk away from the table if the offer, salary, job, or requirements don't fit into your needs, your life, or your goals. Sometimes, when you don't have anything to lose, you can make your best argument, and knowing that you have the power and strength to walk away is the most empowering thing of all.

A lot of people ask my advice about negotiating a counteroffer.

Picture this, you have a job; you are not feeling the love. You either don't get paid what you believe you are worth; you and your boss are not on the same page; you hate the hours, the commute, the product, or your peers. There are a million different reasons why people leave jobs.

Most of us cannot afford to be without a paycheck for very long, so most of us look for a new job while we still have one.

You polish up the resume, you start interviewing, and before long, you have an offer. Say your offer is $25,000 more than you are making now. Excited and thrilled to be out of the job you dislike, you gleefully give your two-weeks' notice.

After that, one of three things are going to happen.

First, like a lot of companies, your current employer tells you to pack up and leave that day. While you may be required to give two-weeks' notice, they don't have to let you work it out. They do have to pay you for it (if it is required), so some people are given the opportunity to clean out their desk, say goodbye to their peers, and take the next the weeks off.

Some people are treated like common criminals. HR sends security to your office to watch you clean out your desk and make sure you don't steal any company trade secrets or the box of paperclips that have been languishing in your desk drawer for the past seven years, and they walk you out of the building in a great "walk of shame" episode.

Second, they let you work out your two weeks' notice, and they may even have a nice going-away party for you. During this time, you will transition your work to other people, but with one foot already out the door, most of your time will be spent cleaning up, cleaning out, and moving on.

Third, your current company gives you a counteroffer. What is a counteroffer, you ask? Well, it is an offer that your company makes to keep you. After treating you like a red-headed step-child for several years, or being a pretty good company to work for, your notice made them think; "Holy hell, we cannot afford to lose this person, so we need to get our shit together and see if we can get them to stay." So, they may offer to match your new job offer; they may offer you a promotion; or they may give you a better title, work arrangement, or company parking spot.

Ultimately, the choice is up to you. But remind yourself there is a reason you are leaving in the first place. 99% if the time, I recommend not accepting a counteroffer. But either way, make sure you receive the best possible offer you can.

> Learning how to ask for, and get, what you want is a skill that will serve you well your entire life.

18 | It's Hard to Be a Woman, So Start a Business

The allure of the female form has captivated humanity for as long as our species has existed. The female face has been responsible for launching ships and starting wars. It has been the face of revolution, societal movements, widespread uprisings, resistance and rebellion against governments, and equality rights advancements for thousands of years. Women are viewed as objects of desire, fierce competitors, great protectors, and a soft place to land.

How can all these elements be seamlessly encapsulated, unified, and characterized as a singular entity? One individual? Women have long bore the burden of being all things to all people.

We must be attractive but not enough to make other women jealous.

We must be beautiful, but not threatening.

We must be smart, but not smarter than our male counterparts.

We must be empathetic, kind, compassionate, but not weak.

We must be powerful, but not aggressive.

We must be good mothers, good friends, good partners, good daughters, good siblings, and good humans, but we shouldn't expect any platitudes, praise, or rewards for our efforts.

If this describes how you feel about being a woman at work or at home, you are not alone. A woman is expected to embody the qualifies of femininity, vulnerability, and grace.

If you work a full-time job, you are also expected to work another full-time one at home, especially if you have children, a spouse, or others to take care of.

Being a woman is exhausting. So many expectations, so little time.

When I first started working in corporate America, the "Me Too" movement was not even a thought. Sexism, inappropriate touching, unprofessional behaviors, and questionable thoughts, feelings, actions, and words toward women were often accepted without thought or fear of retaliation by the perpetrator.

I, along with my female peers, was propositioned, grabbed, touched, told dirty jokes, told to "smile" or worse, and there was very little recourse.

If you complained, you were a "problem." There were no safe spaces or support groups, no one came to your defense, and if you were being sexually harassed, you were made to feel like it was your fault. "Don't wear short skirts," don't "entice" men, don't, don't, don't.

Of course, this was the age of "Greed is good," and anyone making money for a company was considered untouchable.

Don't get me wrong. Females were presented with opportunities in the workplace that our mothers could only dream about, but along with the good, there was the bad, and the conversations around harassment were bottled up and presented in annual "sexual harassment" trainings that were mandatory and forgotten once everyone left the room.

Lip service to female equality was rampant, but real-life equality was hard to find. We saw high-profile cases brought to the forefront during those years. Anita Hill, a respected law professor, accused Clarence Thomas of sexual harassment, and he still was appointed to the U.S. Supreme Court. Paula Jones accused Bill Clinton of the same. He remained president.

So, despite their accusations, testimonies, and loss of anonymity, the efforts of many women to expose sexual harassment resulted in nothing more than cursory acknowledgment that "maybe this is a problem."

Of course, all of that changed in 2017 when *Me Too* became a household term, and women, in droves, began stepping forward with their horror stories of the pervasiveness of harassment, assault, and attacks in the workplace and beyond.

We found community in each other's stories, in each other's experiences. We found enlightenment and power in each other's bravery, and we found kindred spirits in the women who were courageous enough to come forward and fight for change.

As of 2023, women hold 50.04% of all jobs in the United States. In 2019, it was 57.4%.

Post-pandemic, there are 7% fewer women in the workplace.

Why? Because working mothers left the workplace in droves when their kids were attending virtual school. Because caretaking primarily still falls to women, and the cost of daycare is prohibitive for many families, so moms (and some dads) stay home with the kids.

Out of 500 possible CEO roles in Fortune 500 companies, there are 74 women CEOs. That is a dismal number despite society's lip service to inclusion and equal opportunities for females in the workplace.

- 75% of self-employed women love their job.
- Only 27.1% of women are managers and leaders.
- 61% of women think motherhood disrupts their progress opportunities.
- On average, women earn 16% less than their male peers.

So, what do you do if you want to be a successful, happy, and well-paid woman in the workplace?

Let's start with business ownership.

According to 2023 workplace survey, 75% of self-employed female entrepreneurs LOVE their jobs! I suspect that this ties into the idea that most women are the main caregivers in their families. As an entrepreneur or self-employed professional, your time, your schedule, and your work-life balance are all your own making. The pressure to show up at a certain time, commute, stay late, or if you call in sick when your child gets sick can be highly stressful.

When you work for yourself, other than having to reschedule the occasional meeting or take a Zoom call with a sick baby in your lap, you can arrange, rearrange, and manage your own time.

There are currently 12 million female-owned business in the United States.

If you want to leave the corporate rat race, own your own time, and be your own boss, what should you do? We have worked with thousands of women who've become business owners, independent consultants, and entrepreneurs. Here is how to get started.

Women can pursue a wide range of business ownership ideas, and the key is to identify your passions, skills, and interests, and then consider how you can turn them into a profitable business.

First, what are you good at? This is not a loaded question. Women are good at a great many things, but being able to define your skills, passions, and experiences, and turn that into a business, can be exciting, but also a challenge.

Questions to ask yourself must include:

Do I consider myself to be adept or an expert in something?
Is there a market for my ideas?
Would someone be willing to pay me for this work?
Could I afford to leave my job or work part-time as I get this off the ground?

So, whether you are a great cook, and start a cooking school, or you are an IT wizard, and start an IT consulting business, you are capable of doing anything you want to do!

Here are some of the most popular entrepreneurial ventures for women in the United States.

E-commerce Store: Start an online store selling products that align with your interests or expertise. You can be a reseller, distributor or wholesaler of homemade or purchased goods. You can use platforms like Shopify, Etsy, or Amazon to set up your online shop.

Consulting Services: I always used to say, "I want to be a consultant when I grow up!" Consulting sounds so important and exciting. So, if you too would like to be a consultant, first figure out what you are an expert in when it comes to business. If it is management, then hang your shingle and become a management consultant where you help companies shore up their leadership team. If you are great at HR, you could offer your services to small businesses in need of HR functions and programs. If you are great at sales, you could be a sales consultant—either offering direct selling talent, or building sales programs for companies who are struggling with keeping, retaining, or motivating their sales teams.

If you have expertise in a particular field, such as marketing, finance, or training, consider offering consulting services to businesses in need of your skills.

If you love working out, are a dedicated fitness fanatic, or love to help people lose weight or get in shape, become a personal trainer, yoga instructor, or wellness coach. You can offer virtual or in-person sessions, develop online courses, and create fitness or wellness products.

Event Planning: If you held legendary birthday parties for your kids, have planned more than one friend's wedding or are the neighborhood "go to" for summer parties and festivals, start an event-planning business. This could include weddings, corporate events, or parties. There is huge money in planning corporate events, and the exposure, travel, and networking opportunities are endless.

Writing or Content Creation: If you've written content, come from a marketing background, or are just a creative person, freelance writing or content creation might be for you. Social media content managers can make hundreds of thousands of dollars annually creating website content, social media posts, or online blogs.

Food Business: If you're a talented cook or baker, start a catering business, food truck, or sell homemade goods like jams, sauces, or baked goods. Mrs. Fields started a cookie baking business, landed in over 100 countries, and ended up selling her business for $100 million dollars. There is money in flour, dough, and sugar.

IT Consultant: Are you a techie? Always fixing everyone's computers, laptops, and phones? IT consultants can make upward of $100,000 annually, more if you are an expert in software management or large technology transformation or implementation projects. I had a client who started as an ER nurse and ended up becoming a super user for their patient management software. She was so good at teaching others to use it that the company offered her a consulting role to lead large-scale project integrations all over the world.

Home Renovation and Interior Design: As an avowed HGTV addict, I admire any woman who can take a few knickknacks from T.J. Maxx and turn their home into a showpiece. During the pandemic, Do It Yourself became a national pastime, and from someone who hired an interior designer to redo her 20-year-old house from top to bottom, I can tell you it is a lucrative line of work. If you have an eye for design, start a business focused on home renovation or interior design services.

And the list goes on and on and on . . . subscription box services, childcare or elderly care services, pet sitting/pet walking services, fashion and beauty, online education.

Remember that the success of any business idea depends on factors like market demand, competition, and your dedication to building and growing the business. It can also depend on dumb luck, being in the right place at the right time, and jumping on a hot new trend.

So, what if entrepreneurship is not for you? How do you, as a woman, succeed in the workplace?

As a woman who has worked in corporate America, been an entrepreneur, and had thousands of female clients, here is my advice.

Stick together. I love all those memes and videos on social media where women have each other's backs. Whether it's telling another woman they look beautiful, borrowing or giving another gal a tampon, offering to take a picture of a "girls night out" group of strangers, or warning another woman about a bad guy, a spiked drink, or an overpriced pair of shoes, women are your best advocates.

For too long, women saw other women as competitors in the workplace, when they needed to be seen as peers, allies, friends, and advocates. There is power in numbers. There is power in sisterhood.

If you can, establish or support existing mentorship programs within your organization where experienced women can mentor younger or less-experienced female colleagues. Many women remember and appreciate the female executives who came before them, especially how they showed them the ropes, gave advice on promotions, who were the best bosses, or the juiciest projects to work on.

Create or participate in women's networking groups within or outside of your workplace. These groups can provide opportunities for women to connect, share experiences, and collaborate, fostering a sense of community and empowerment. As a business owner, I belong to many networking groups, and through them, I've found new staff members, great ideas, and connections where I can make introductions for my resume clients.

Encourage the sharing of skills and knowledge among women in the workplace. If you see someone struggling, offer a hand. Petition your leadership for workshops or informal training sessions where women can teach each other valuable skills, whether they relate to leadership, technical expertise, or personal development. A great ally within your workplace is your learning and development department. Its job is to create learning and training opportunities that benefit not only the company, but the employees as well. I once had a client who started off working in a help desk role. She took every single available training, found a kindred soul within the learning and development department to bring on more and more IT training/courses/certifications, and now she is an IT executive.

"See something, say something" is the best way to phrase this next idea. Women talk. We have friends in HR, we have friends in management, we have friends in the workplace. And we also chat, like to share stories, and, okay, we do a bit of gossiping. There is nothing juicier than finding out a male peer makes twice as much as his female counterpart. Whether it is just too good NOT to talk about, or women really want to see others succeed, that bit of information is highly likely to get out. If you know of that type of situation, and at no detriment to yourself, let a fellow female know she's being under-cut. What she does with that information will be up to her, but ultimately, when women speak up and speak out against salary inequality, it is better for everyone.

If you are in leadership, create opportunities and influence management to select qualified women for other leadership roles. When women advocate for other women to get promotions, that is laying the foundation for more women in leadership roles. Support and nominate qualified women for leadership positions and actively participate in discussions on diversity and inclusion.

I was hanging out at a restaurant/bar on the Jersey Shore, and there was a woman seated across from me on the outside patio with an incredible pair of tie-up wedge sandals. My daughter and I kept looking at them, and wondering where she got them, what the name brand was, and how much they cost. You know, typical stuff we gals do all the time. Anyway, at the end of the evening as she walked out, she passed our table, and I stopped her. I said, "We've been admiring your shoes all night and you look beautiful!" She gasped in surprise, smiled so widely, and reached down to hug me. We embraced and wished each other a fantastic rest of the evening. I said to my daughter, "This is the power of a compliment. We so often are harried, stressed, overworked, and underappreciated, that a few kind words between females can be an incredibly empowering thing." I make it a daily habit to find someone to compliment. Whether it is a woman on my team, a stranger in the grocery store, or a group of women at a restaurant, I find myself saying "You women look gorgeous" or "I love your hair." Try it, see what happens.

At work, you should celebrate the achievements and successes of your female colleagues. You can take a page from the Taylor Swift/Selena Gomez book . . . I love that relationship and how they cheer for one another, stick up for each other, and hate on ex-boyfriends publicly who did them dirty.

> Glass ceilings are made to be broken.

19 | Recruiters Hate Me; I Am Okay with That

Let me preface this chapter by saying that I count many recruiters and headhunters as friends, allies, and resources for our resume clients, and many of these folks are good, hard-working, and respectable people. If you follow me on LinkedIn, you know that I have a bug up my craw for negligent, ignorant, lazy, and rude recruiting processes and recruiters.

I am by no means saying that recruiting is not a hard job. So many candidates, so little time, and all that. But my biggest pet peeve in the hiring process is lack of communication and rude, disinterested, or inconsiderate people, and that is mostly aimed at recruiters who drop the ball, string people along, and treat them like dog doodoo instead of worthy candidates.

Recruiters get blamed for a lot of the ghosting that happens in the interview process, and rightly so. It is their job to keep candidates informed, it is their job to maintain open levels of communication, and it is their job to let you know that you did not get the position so you can move on. While I do, from time to time, understand that recruiters can feel overwhelmed, just like the rest of us, I do not believe there is any valid excuse to ignore any candidate who has, in good faith, put in the time and effort to go through an interview process.

So, that said, many of my LinkedIn posts are designed to communicate how important it is that candidates feel seen, valued, and heard throughout the hiring process, and when the ball gets dropped, it is typically the recruiter's fault.

Quite often, I get notes from recruiters telling me that I am being unfair to them, that their jobs are hard, and oftentimes, when a candidate has not been informed about their status, it's because someone at the company has not made a decision, NOT them.

But I say "Hogwash!" to that excuse. Even if a decision has not been made, the recruiter needs to be the ally to the candidate, not the enemy. If you are involved in the communication process, but you've got nothing to report, it's okay. Just let the candidate know.

It is the glaring lack of transparency that gives recruiters a bad name. Some candidates feel that recruiters are not transparent about job details, salary ranges, or the hiring process. This lack of clarity can lead to misunderstandings and wasted time for candidates. Anyone who is looking for a new position is on a time crunch. They are either without a job or anxious to leave their existing one, for a variety of reasons regardless of the situation. So, when a job seeker launches a job search, there is usually a sense of urgency that cannot be denied. When a recruiter doesn't acknowledge or understand that, it causes a problem. My clients or perfect strangers on LinkedIn let me know, then I call out the bad practice, and thousands of people chime in with their own terrible experiences. This is not an isolated problem or the experience of just a few. Fundamentally, it is this lack of respect for the candidate's time that makes people angry. No one is upset that they didn't get the job. Everyone is upset if they've been ignored.

Candidates become frustrated when recruiters do not respond to their emails, phone calls, or questions. Poor communication creates uncertainty and anxiety during the job search, at a time when there is anxiety and uncertainty in droves. A simple phone call or email that says "They have not made a decision yet" or "You are still in the running" could solve so many issues, yet it seems sometimes that even that is too difficult to get.

Not long ago, a recruiter reached out to me by email and asked if I was interested in learning more about a chief human resources officer role in my area. She said she found my resume online and thought I'd be a great fit for the role. Now, I have not had a resume in 20+ years (trust me, I see the irony here), so first, that was a lie. She did not see my resume anywhere. Second, even if she saw my profile online, I've owned a business for 24 years and have not had an HR title in decades. What in the world would make someone think I was looking for a job?

I normally just delete those emails, but on this day, I was feeling particularly feisty and emailed her back. "Thanks for your note, but I am not remotely interested in a job. I own a very successful business and have owned this business for 24 years. I am not sure what about me, my experience, or my information would lead you to send this to me, but I suggest that you do several things. First, vet your target's experience before you blast out your emails, and second, don't lie about having someone's resume. I do not have a resume listed online, on any job board, and have not applied for a job in 25 years. All the best to you."

She did not respond. But this belies a common problem in the recruitment process. Recruiters present job opportunities that are not aligned with the candidate's skills, experience, or career goals. This is both frustrating and insulting for candidates who feel their time is wasted on irrelevant opportunities.

Of all the things that lead to extraordinary job seeker frustration is the lack of follow-up. Less than 50% of job seekers report that they receive an appropriate amount of follow-up after participating in an interview. Just half. Let that sink in. Candidates dislike recruiters who promise to follow up but fail to do so, so much so that it gives the entire industry of recruitment a bad name. While I can understand that not every job applicant gets a response (which still seems crazy to me since those can be automated), every single person who has gone through an interview should get some sort of response. It can be as simple as "It was great to meet you, we are moving forward with other candidates at this time. We wish you all the best." That's it. Candidates are not looking for a book, a lengthy explanation, or even a phone call. A simple email would solve this issue, but alas, even that seems to be asking too much.

I have heard countless stories of candidates who have interviewed multiple times, filled out lengthy applications, participated in interview homework such as the development of business plans, marketing plans, strategy or data assessments, taken personality and skills tests, and have been strung along for months only to come to find out through the grapevine that the job was filled, put on hold, or canceled altogether. That is what makes job seekers angry, and they should be. A blatant disrespect for people's time, brain power, and preparation needs to be appreciated and valued, not ignored.

So, check out Chapter 20 on ghosting and try out those three questions at the end of the chapter in your next interview opportunity and hopefully you will see a change.

It's important to note that these frustrations are not representative of all recruiters, and many recruiters prioritize candidate satisfaction and strive to provide a positive experience. They are the most successful recruiters. Building trust between candidates and recruiters is essential for a successful hiring process and should be the norm, not the exception.

Candidates should also consider working with reputable recruiters and agencies to increase the likelihood of a positive experience.

What sort of recruiter should you be looking for?

There are three different kinds of recruiters.

1. **In-house recruiters:** This is a recruiter who is employed by the company to fill internal positions. Their job is to identify, attract, and hire qualified candidates to fill job vacancies within the company. I believe this is the best kind of recruiter. They are paid a salary, and maybe a bonus based on performance, but they have the time, resources, and availability to vet candidates, provide ongoing communication about the process, and see a candidate through the initial interview to the offer. They may also

be involved in onboarding processes as well as handling employment contracts. While there is a bit of urgency in all hiring, there is less pressure on internal recruiters to fill jobs quickly, and that allows for a more qualified process, better communication, and a more enjoyable experience.

2. **Headhunters:** A headhunter is an executive recruiter or search consultant who specializes in identifying and recruiting highly qualified candidates for senior-level, executive, or specialized positions within organizations. Headhunters also focus on C-suite candidates and have been known to "poach" C-suite talent from a company's competitor to fill a role. These searches tend to be fairly secretive in nature, and many headhunters will not divulge to a candidate the name of the employer until well into the search. Most jobs that headhunters focus on are high-level or sensitive, as in someone is getting fired and their replacement is being "headhunted" before they are let go. Most of the jobs that headhunters focus on are critical to the organization and their leadership teams. Headhunters operate independently on a contingency/placement fee basis and have been hired/contracted by a company to fill a role. They work for themselves, not the company, and their fees often exceed 20% to 30% of the candidate's first-year's salary as compensation for filling that role.

Headhunters manage their own schedules, are trusted to maintain a high level of secrecy, and they often target candidates who are not actively looking for a new job. If you get a call from a headhunter, take it seriously. If they are calling, they are willing to woo you and win you over with a compelling offer. Most successful headhunters have an extensive network of contacts within their industry or specialization. We have resume clients who have had 20-year relationships with headhunters who often recommend them or contact them for new opportunities whenever those opportunities arise.

Headhunters will be your first line of defense to get into a lucrative executive level role. They will run you through the paces, ensuring you are both technically qualified as well as have the experience, attitude, and are the right cultural fit for the client organization.

You will go through in-depth interviews, reference checks, and sometimes psychological assessments. Your headhunter will assist you in negotiating a compensation package. The more you make, the more THEY make, so it is in their best interest to get you the best offer.

Building a long-term relationship with both companies and candidate is their bread and butter. A really great headhunter can help you and other candidates build and advance your career over a long period of time.

3. **Contract Recruiters:** A contract recruiter typically fills lower-level positions, but not entry level. They may or MAY NOT have a relationship with the company they are looking to present you to. Be cautious of recruiters who do not have an affiliation or relationship with an employer for a specific position. Oftentimes, independent or contract recruiters may identify a potential job opportunity, and independently identify candidates who might fill that role. Then, once they vet you, deem you to be an appropriate candidate, they may use YOU as their "in" with an organization to establish a relationship. These situations typically do not end well. If you've been contacted by a contract recruiter, and they cannot gain any traction or a foothold into a company, you won't hear back from them. They are not interested in your career growth or job search success; they are interested in leveraging you for their own opportunities.

The takeaway here is to ask the following questions when a recruiter or headhunter reaches out to you.

1. Are you employed by the company you are recruiting for?
2. Are you contracted by the company you are recruiting for?
3. Are you able to share the salary range, job title, and job description?
4. What is the timeline for this position to be filled?

And that's it! The best way to deal with recruiters and head-hunters is to build a trustworthy and informative relationship. They could pave the way for a new opportunity.

A recruiter can be a friend or foe; navigate with care.

20 | Casper the Unfriendly Ghost

A major issue in the modern job search is something called *ghosting*. You've probably heard the term. It started off as a social term that originally gained attention in the context of dating and personal relationships, but has since been extended to other contexts, including professional and business settings. And now, it describes what happens to candidates in the interview process.

Ghosting in a job search happens when either a job candidate or an employer suddenly stops responding or providing updates during the recruitment process.

This is a new thing that has happened over the course of the past decade, as anyone who conducted a job search previous to this "ghosting epidemic" can tell you.

Back in the day, employers, for the most part, were pretty good at letting you know that you didn't get the job. They'd always followed up with a call or email, thanking you for your time, and letting you know they'd keep your resume on file for future opportunities.

Who can forget the little postcards that came in the mail letting you know your application was received, but you were not being considered for the role. That was a nice touch. It did not leave you in limbo, and you felt valued and appreciated for your application.

But now, ghosting is completely out of control. Not only do they not let you know your application is/is not being considered, many times, you don't even get a response when you've interviewed—whether it is once or multiple times.

It is highly frustrating and unprofessional, and it often leaves job seekers feeling very jaded about their processes and potential prospects. I've seen candidates ghosted so much that they've left the job search process altogether and have taken jobs well beneath their educational and experience level, or started businesses because they just could not go through one more interview process.

Overcoming this ghosting epidemic takes creativity, patience, and persistence.

When you are being ghosted in an interview process, especially if you are out of work, exhausted from the job search, or you've been ghosted more than once, it's extremely easy to lose your cool. That is an absolutely valid way to feel, and job seekers deserve respect, open communication, and information along the way.

Here is how to handle or avoid being ghosted.

1. When you engage in the interview process, before you even say "yes" to the interview, ask these three questions:
    - How long/how many interviews will be conducted before a hiring decision is made?
    - What is the salary range for this position?
    - When is the targeted start date for this role?

When you get this information up front, you can make the call as to whether or not you wish to proceed. Red flags to look out for include:

   - Anything over three touches is going to be a mess.
   - They don't have a salary range.
   - They don't have a start date.

I find that if they cannot answer these questions, there are several things going on. First, they are fishing to see how cheaply they can get someone to fill the role. Or, if they don't have a start date in mind, it is not an urgent situation, and it could be many months before they are ready to make an offer or they may not fill the role at all. We recently had a client go through a six-interview process and when she was expecting the offer, she was told that after talking to so many candidates, they were rethinking/reframing the job and it is put on hold indefinitely. So, they wasted the time of 10+ people, multiple interviews, each to determine that they did not need this job filled at all.

Another big red flag is salary. All jobs have a range assigned to them. No exceptions. No one makes this stuff up as they go along. If an employer is not willing to share a general range, they are doing one of two things: (1) They either did not put the legwork into determining an attractive salary to attract the best people or (2) they are going to spitball the offer. Which means, they are going to throw some offer out there to see what sticks. It is a very cheap and lazy way of getting the candidate to do the work for you. For example, they think this might be a $120,000-a-year job, but they interview a decent candidate, and if that candidate is willing to take $95,000, that becomes what the job pays.

This is a bad idea for everyone involved. Eventually, in the not-too-distant future, the person hired is going to realize that they are not getting paid what they are worth, and also the company has just driven down salaries for hires that come after whoever accepted this offer. Even if the person who originally accepted the $95,000 offer stays for one year, the next person to come along to apply for this job won't be getting a fair, market value driven offer. They will be getting the $95,000 benchmark.

2. If you've participated in multiple interviews and the time in which you were told there would be a follow-up has come and gone, reach out. I recommend one email and one phone call. Give it a few days and see if anyone follows up with you. Be cordial, be nice, be professional in all your communication.

If you do not hear anything back, they either have not decided if you are moving forward or no one on the team is mature enough to call you and tell you that you did not get the job. I see this as a very common problem in the hiring process. Everyone is busy, but it is not an excuse to ghost a candidate. Candidates put a ton of time, effort, legwork, and preparation into preparing for the requirements, so the least you can do is give them a quick call or a thoughtful email.

Once you've left the message, once you've sent the email. Give it a week. Then do this . . .

Call/email the contact person you've engaged with throughout the process. In your message say these words. "I am extremely disappointed that despite being told that I would hear from your office, I have yet to receive a call or email regarding the status of this job. At this time, while I am still interested in the position, I am actively engaged with other potential employers for other opportunities. If I do not hear back from you either by phone or email at the close of business on Friday [or pick your day], please remove my candidacy from consideration for this role, and confirm that you have done so."

In my experience, 95% of the time, you will hear back in four hours or less. The next day at the latest.

Why does this work? First, no one wants to hear that anyone is disappointed. Second, if you are still being considered and they can't seem to make a decision, they will want to keep you on the hook. If you are NOT still being considered, you've opened the door for them to let you off the hook, and you look like the "bad guy," not them.

3. At the end of your very first interview with the company, when they ask, "Do you have any questions?" ask these three things:
   - Who will be my point of contact during this process?
   - When do you expect to reach out to me to let me know the next steps?
   - If I do not hear from you at the designated follow up, do you prefer that I contact you by phone or email?

This is what I call the "holding-someone's-feet-to-the-fire" approach. When you ask these questions, expect clear answers, and if they agree or confirm these answers, it would be difficult to ignore you without looking like a fool!

While interviewing can be an exhausting, intensive, and highly involved process, you are not powerless. You can stop interviewing at any time. You can position yourself to be "kept in the loop," and you can do your best to ensure that your efforts are not overlooked or ignored. If you do find yourself in a situation where you have not and cannot get an answer or a response, move on. While it is disappointing to be ignored, you are a strong, resilient, and smart professional, and you deserve both respect and acknowledgment of your value.

> Be too good to be ignored.

21

To Cover Letter or Not to Cover Letter, That Is the Question

If you've conducted a job search at any point in the past decade, or plan to conduct one soon, you should ask yourself the age-old question: "Should I include a cover letter?"

And the answer is, "It depends."

In a world of information overload, very long job applications, and a bevy of other obstacles to obtaining employment, asking a frustrated, exhausted, and overloaded job seeker to provide MORE information seems a bit cruel.

I mean, how much more information does someone need? They have your resume, they've viewed your LinkedIn profile, they have your application, where you systematically fill out all the information FROM your resume to their online portal. You've filled out all the dates, the jobs, your college graduation dates, your employment history, your blood type and vaccination status. For God's sake, how much more do they want from you?

Well, sometimes they want a cover letter.

Here are the rules of thumb:

- If you've logged into a company website or online job portal, and you've uploaded your resume and there is a space for a cover letter, and you cannot bypass the page without including one, you must include it. If you can bypass it, do. Don't include it.
- If you email your resume to a contact or someone you've been introduced to, do NOT include a cover letter. Write a nice little note or email instead. Make sure you name drop the person who introduced you, why you are interested in the job, and any other relevant information to your note. Don't write a book. Write two paragraphs and call it a day.
- If you set up a job search alert on a company's careers page, upload a general cover letter that highlights your most recent experiences, job titles, nature of the position you are after, and why you might be interested in working for them.

    If you REALLY want the job, think you are a great fit, list three separate bullets on the cover letter that shows a direct correlation between your experience and something specific they are asking for in the job requisition or job description.
- For any cover letter you do submit, keep it short. I know you have a lot to say, but in the age of information overload, a short, succinct cover letter will be appreciated. And maybe even read by someone.

While a well-crafted cover letter can significantly increase your chances of landing that dream interview, tailoring a cover letter to every single job you apply for can be a time suck.

A cover letter should be a one-page document that accompanies your resume when applying for a job. I favor shorter cover letters, two to three paragraphs at most. It provides an opportunity to introduce yourself, highlight your qualifications, and explain why you are an excellent fit for the position and the company. Think of it as your sales pitch to the employer.

The more you can personalize it, the better. Know someone who works for the company? Name drop and talk about how they love the organization. Have a passion for the company's mission or product? Share your own personal story about why. Used the company's products? Talk about that. A genuine story about how you relate to the organization, its product, or its culture is always going to be better than a generic approach.

Before you start writing, you need to gather essential information and create a plan for your cover letter. Start by reading, and then rereading the job description/job requirements. Select three very specific things the company requires, and then tell a little ditty about how your experience relates.

For instance, say you are applying for a director of sales role for a global company based in Spain. If you speak conversational Spanish, have traveled to Spain, or have specific knowledge of the company's targeted market, talk about that.

Or, if you are applying to a job where one of the requirements is knowledge of a specific kind of software or system tool, and you are a super user, say that in your cover letter.

It is important to identify your key selling points as they relate to the job, but telling a great story of success you've had in a previous role is always going to be better than just saying "I have experience in this or that."

When you are addressing your cover letter, try to find the hiring manager or recruiter's name. Everyone prefers to read a cover letter addressed to them specifically, as opposed to "To whom it may concern." If you cannot find a name, I suggest that you just leave that portion of the cover letter blank.

Now that you have your resume ready to go, your cover letter written, you should apply to as many jobs as you can find. When it all comes down to it, a job search is a numbers game. The more you apply, the more interviews you get, the better your chances of landing that dream job!

Here is a great example of a cover letter:

Date

Name

Title

Company Name

Address

City, State ZIP

Dear Mr./Ms. Name,

It is with considerable interest that I submit my resume in response to the [Position Title] position posted on the [Company Name] website. My background demonstrates a proven record of evaluating, negotiating, and closing large-scale deals that grow the brand footprint, navigating through complex legal and business issues in contracts to find win–win solutions for all parties involved. I define the right rules of engagement and deal structures to align global brands with the right set of partners to propel business success.

Moreover, I leverage astute negotiation ability with strategic contract drafting to secure some of Amazon's most crucial partner alliances and support the extraordinary evolution of XXX technology. I utilize substantial skills in analyzing data to provide actionable insights that achieve consensus among executive and functional stakeholders. With a demonstrated capacity to develop and lead high-performance teams, I combine individual capabilities with effective team leadership to deliver exceptional results.

Specific career achievements include:

- Individually evaluated, negotiated, and closed 100% of required deals to launch XXX Local Information in United States and Canada (3 deals), Italy (1 deal), Japan (2 deals), India (1 deal), Brazil (1 deal), and Mexico (1 deal).
- Provided astute leadership and coaching to Business Development team members who signed 100% of required deals to launch additional customer features in United States and

Canada (4 deals), multiple EU countries (2 deals), and India (3 deals).

- Orchestrated all aspects of opportunities from financial evaluation, pipeline management, contract negotiation, signing, and scoping/oversight of operations implementation—involved 14 internal teams.

Enclosed is my resume, which provides a more in-depth view of my qualifications and expertise. I hope to schedule an interview to learn more about your needs and expectations, and provide you with more insight into what I offer. Please contact me at your earliest convenience to set up a time for us to speak. Thank you for your time and consideration.

I look forward to hearing from you soon.

Sincerely,

Name

> A cover letter is the story you tell before your resume begins to speak.

22

Tell Me about Yourself

You've been applying for jobs for weeks or months. You've customized your resume, filled out endless online applications, written more cover letters than you thought possible, networked, asked for introductions, and taken a variety of skills and personality assessments, all with the hope of getting an interview.

Finally, the day comes, and a recruiter or HR representative reaches out to you to schedule an interview. You are excited, a little nervous, and prepared to make an impression, sound intelligent, and hopefully, win a job offer.

It sounds easy enough, right?

You put on our Sunday best, arrive early, bring a few paper copies of your resume, and wait for the interview to begin. After ushering you to the interview location, you are greeted, exchange pleasantries, and are ready to get down to business.

The first question the interviewer asks is, "Tell me about yourself."

You freeze up, mumble through your answer, and your palms start to sweat. Your brain is racing a thousand miles a minute. Do they want information about your personal or professional life?

You wrack your brain for something smart to say and end up telling them about how you helped your previous employer save thousands of dollars/how you contributed to their success/or how you won "employee of the year."

That is the best-case scenario.

Worst case? You tell some inane story about how you met your spouse on a dating app or how you recently lost 30 pounds.

Either way, open-ended questions like this are the equivalent of throwing a bottle rocket into a crowd to see who ducks and runs, or who tries to save their mother.

I once had a resume client who was a marketing executive and new mother. She had left her old job once she found out she was pregnant, took the year off, and by the time the baby was three months old, was ready to go back to work. She was interested in exploring other marketing executive roles, and during her time off, she worked on her social media knowledge as well as experiential marketing philosophies. Marketing is one of those fields that is changing constantly, and if you are not keeping up with the latest and greatest trends, you find yourself outside looking in.

She was anxious to get back to work in a high-level marketing role where she could flex her knowledge of social media as well as lead a team, drive marketing strategy, and work with a company where she could eventually move into a chief marketing officer role.

We worked with her to make her resume relevant again, got rid of outdated marketing language, talked about things she learned and studied during her time off, captured her last 10+ years of work experience, and added as many metrics/measurable outcomes from her marketing efforts as possible.

When developing a function specific resume, which is a resume that is geared toward the same type of role someone has already had, we do a 10-point keyword analysis to capture the top 10 things that someone might be looking for in their candidate. In this case, a resume for a marketing executive is going to contain highlights of the most common keywords and functions for a marketing executive: I am listing out a few examples of what we covered, but you can do this for any function by comparing keywords in job postings that you are interested in.

Strategic Planning: Emphasize your ability to develop and execute strategic marketing plans.

Leadership: Highlight your experience in leading marketing teams and projects.

Digital Marketing: Showcase your expertise in various digital marketing channels, such as SEO, SEM, content marketing, email marketing, and social media.

Data Analysis: Mention your proficiency in analyzing marketing data and using insights to make *informed* decisions.

Brand Management: Emphasize your experience in building, maintaining, and enhancing brand equity.

Campaign Management: Highlight your skills in planning and managing marketing campaigns from concept to execution.

ROI (Return on Investment): Demonstrate your ability to measure and maximize the ROI of marketing efforts.

Market Research: Mention your expertise in conducting market research and using consumer insights to inform marketing strategies.

Product Launch: If applicable, showcase your experience in successfully launching new products or services.

Cross-Functional Collaboration: Communicate your ability to work effectively with other departments, such as sales, product development, and IT, to achieve marketing goals.

After we worked with her on her resume, she sent it to a media company that she had long admired and was excited to learn more about. She got called for an interview, invited her mom to watch the baby, and traveled from Connecticut to New York City to take the meeting. In all fairness, I think she was just as excited about being out of the house for a day as she was to meet with the interviewer.

That day, she prepared for her interview by squeezing into a favorite pre-pregnancy dress, lining her bra with nursing pads and trying to find her career mojo by entering the room with her old self-confidence and spirit. And a great pair of high heels, which made her feel powerful and beautiful.

She was greeted by a lovely HR executive who stood behind the desk and reached out to shake her hand. As my client reached across the desk, with her purse still on her arm, she knocked over the woman's cup of coffee, sending the liquid all over the place. It splashed on them both; she apologized profusely, began sweating, and tried to regain her composure.

To her credit, she did collect herself. She took a few deep breaths, proceeded with the interview, and answered a series of questions. She explained her recent employment gap, talked a bit about her baby, and her desire to return to work.

At one point, she looked down and the front of her dress was soaked with milk. She doesn't know if it was her nervousness or something else, but her breasts had leaked, and she spent the remainder of the interview trying to nonchalantly cover herself with her tablet.

When she got back to her car, she cried. Then she laughed. Then she called me, and we laughed together.

She did NOT get the job offer; in fact, they let her know nearly immediately she was no longer in contention for the role. It only goes to show you that even the most polished, the most prepared and the most professional of candidates can sometimes have an off day when it comes to interviewing.

But for her, it was a lesson in humility, but it also reinforced the fact that she was ready to go back to work. Despite the spilled coffee, leaky breasts, and embarrassing scenario, she was just as jazzed to continue her search, and find the role that fit perfectly along with her new title as mom.

If this had happened to me, I probably wouldn't have taken another interview for a year, but she got right back in the saddle and within two months, she accepted a new position. One that worked for her.

If interviewing wasn't stressful enough, it often comes with odd-ball questions. Why do interviewers ask these oddball questions? Well, first, they are trying to see how you think on your feet, and second, they are looking for problem-solving abilities, character traits, and red flags for how you might react to quirky situations.

I am personally not a huge fan of strange interview questions. To me, it seems like a bit of a "gotcha" approach, whereas I would much rather get a genuine feel for candidates based on good, old-fashioned conversations rather than trickery.

But I am going to share with you some of the questions our clients have gotten over the years and the reasons they get asked of candidates in an interview.

- "If you were a fruit, what type of fruit would you be, and why?"

This is to assess a candidate's ability to think metaphorically.

- "If you were stranded on a deserted island and could only bring three items, what would they be?"

This is a critical-thinking and survival question. They are looking to see how quickly you can assess a dangerous or drastic situation and what you would prioritize in that setting.

- "How many golf balls can fit in a school bus?"

This speaks to your basic math and estimation skills and shows if you can break down a problem into manageable parts.

- "If you were a superhero, what would your superpower be?"

This is the modern-day equivalent to "What are your strengths?" and shows the interviewer the powers, strengths, and capabilities that you consider to be most important.

- "What's your kindred spirit, and why do you think it represents you?"

I hate this question; it is a bit of self-awareness mumbo jumbo, but it can be fun to see how people draw a parallel.

- "If you could have dinner with any historical figure, who would it be, and what would you ask them?"

Of all the questions listed here, I would say I have used this one the most. I hire people who would want to have dinner with their deceased grandfather over the person who picks Jesus or Abraham Lincoln. I am most attracted to empathetic, compassionate, and family-oriented candidates who share similar values to me.

- And my personal favorite, "If you were a dinosaur, what type of dinosaur would you be?"

This is a fun question for me. First, it tells me if you were paying attention in history and science class, but it also lets me know how you view yourself in a hierarchy. Plus, it is good for a laugh and that is something everyone needs when they are going through an interview.

Most interviewers use something called the STAR method, which I will talk about in the next chapter, but I have learned from both my work in HR and as a business owner, that the more genuine questions you ask, the more genuine your interest in a candidate is, the more you really wish to gain insight into someone's personality, the better you are at hiring people. I think that really great interviewers, great hiring decision-makers, look at candidates' personalities, thoughtfulness, and reactions with more weight than their qualifications.

After all, if you did not meet the criteria, qualifications, or requirements for the job, you would not be sitting in that interview chair.

So, for me, the best interviewer is always the person who is the best judge of character.

I am not going to give you the standard "how to prepare for your interview" advice. You can find that anywhere on the internet. Instead, I am going to share with you some tips and tools for things that have worked for our clients, and specific tidbits that may help you to calm your interview nerves, relate to the person asking the questions, and shine your light in any interview you have.

First the basics. Research the company, know what it does, what it is, what it makes, sells, or promotes. Find recent news about the company; that should include any financial data, any industry trades where it is featured, and any highlights about its leadership team. Go to the company's website, know its tagline/motto, and repeat that in an interview for extra brownie points.

Get your LinkedIn detective cap on and identify key personnel, including the CEO and relevant department heads, and learn about their backgrounds and contributions to the company. If you see the person you are interviewing with on LinkedIn, send them a note and connection request. If they accept or answer, score one for you.

Find out their pain points, where they might be struggling in the market, know who the company's competitors are and how it positions itself in the market.

I once had a client who was fluent in Spanish get a job offer with a major telecom provider who was trying and failing to gain a foothold for new distributors and product sales in South America.

He went into the interview armed with stories about bribing local government officials in Mexico to get permit approval to build a small manufacturing facility for a small mobile device company. Yes, I know what you are going to say. They made it clear during the interview that he would not be expected or supported in doing the same type of thing for them, but HE made it clear that he knew how things worked in certain parts of the world, was familiar with the local politics, and had a deep understanding of the buying habits of consumers in South American countries. He took that gamble and it paid off.

Get insight and clarity on the actual job description for the role you will be interviewing for. Sometimes job descriptions are a mumbo jumbo of word salad, wish lists, and outlandish requirements made up by someone who clearly does not know what this job should be. Try to look past that, to identify the key skills, qualifications, and experiences the role requires.

This will allow you to tailor your responses to showcase how your background aligns with their needs. Always, always, always have three major examples, with measurable results, where you did something similar in a previous job.

For instance, if you are interviewing with a pharmaceutical company for a sales representative position, and you've been a pharma rep before, make sure you can tell stories about drug launches, new product roll-outs, market share capture rates, script counts, revenue, building relationships with key opinion leaders, and who are doctors and other healthcare professionals who will promote your drug for you to their doctor friends. Yes, this is a thing. The more you can speak the lingo of the industry, of the role, of the company, the more likely you are to be looked at as "one of them."

To coffee or not to coffee? When asked, job seekers report that their nerves can often get the best of them when headed to an interview. Sweaty palms, a shaky voice, a shaky handshake, mind going blank, and general overall nervousness have been widely known to cause qualified, capable, and smart candidates to blow an interview.

The more you want the job, the more nervous you can be. Or maybe you have not interviewed in a while. Or maybe this is your last-ditch effort to get out of a toxic workplace, but the interviewing ecosystem has proven to be more of a challenge than your micromanaging boss. Whatever the reason, calm those nerves using these suggestions.

- If your interview is in the morning, have a good breakfast and switch to decaf.
- Coffee can exacerbate even a little bit of nerves, and make your heart race, flush your skin, and make you short of breath. I consider myself to be an expert coffee maker and coffee drinker, and even I sometimes find myself asking, "Am I having a heart attack?" after a particularly strong pot of Major Dickason's dark blend. (If you have not tried Peet's coffee, do yourself a favor and buy a bag.)
- Plan your outfit the day before and have a Plan B just in case. Many people can attest to the fact that they've bought a special outfit, suit, or dress for an occasion, but when the time comes, they just aren't feeling it.
  - Ladies, you know this to be true. You've planned the perfect ensemble, but you are feeling bloated, or it is too hot to put on the shapewear, or those shoes that were so cute when you got them are now hurting your feet. So, I suggest having back-up attire just in case. Something where you still feel confident and powerful, but comfortable too.

- Guys, I don't know about you, but my husband has been known to try seven different ties on with this favorite navy suit, or heaven forbid, spill something on his shirt the minute we are walking out the door to go to a wedding. So, an extra shirt, comfy shoes for your drive, and an alternate tie choice hanging in the closet can make the day of your interview a little less stressful.

- Print out a few copies of your resume to hand out, just in case. Your resume can be used as a guideline to showcase not only your accomplishments, but to remind you of things you want the interviewer to know, hear, or learn from you about your history.

    Since we live in a digital world and most applications are viewed on a screen, many times the interviewer will NOT have a copy of your resume. So, it is nice to bring a few along, just in case. And it's another way to show you are prepared.

Finally, practice, practice, practice. There was a television sitcom in the 1970s called *The Brady Bunch*. A true classic about a family made up of a husband and wife, they each had three kids (the wife, daughters; the husband, sons), and they got married. If you've never seen it, Google it. It still has a cult following, and while it was designed as a heartwarming story about a blended family, it gave the greatest tidbits of life lessons ever known to mankind.

One of the episodes was about one of the daughters who had to give a speech and she was incredibly nervous. She practiced her speech in front of the mirror, and you should do the same. Lock yourself in your bathroom, turn on the lights, and observe how you smile, look, sit, speak, and make eye contact. Practice your elevator pitch. Practice your answers. Practice your three examples of successful job performance stories, and then do it again. The more confident you look and sound, the more confident they will be in you.

In that same episode, her stepfather gave her the best advice, and both hilarity and wisdom ensued. He told her to picture the audience in their underwear to reduce her nervousness, and that is exactly what she did.

Of course, it was a sitcom, so it was made to be funny, but the moral of the story is this: we are all people just trying to do our best and no matter what position someone is in, or what position you are in, we all look funny in our underwear. No, just kidding. The lesson is that we are all equals, and by taking away the idea that someone is judging you and acknowledge that he or she is more like you than you think, that can help to calm your trepidations.

Preparation, research, practice are the three main pillars to interviewing successfully. In the next chapter, I will go into greater details around the most common interview questions and how to put your very best foot forward.

> If you can survive a funny or dumb interview question, you can survive the interview.

23

Be a STAR

You've finally landed the interview! Now what? Well, as you read in the previous chapter, the best way to prepare is to practice, research, and have at least three or four very specific stories about your career successes that you can refer to during the interview. While interviewing can feel like the Wild West, and quite literally anything can happen, the most common method of interviewing today is something called the STAR Method.

STAR stands for Situation, Task, Action, Result, and is one of the most popular forms of behavior-based interviewing.

I am going to give you three specific examples of questions, answers, and how to best prepare for these questions.

Question 1: Can you provide an example of a time when you had to work on a challenging team project with a tight deadline? How did you handle it, and what was the outcome?

Situation: "In my previous role as a project manager at XYZ Company, we were tasked with launching a new product within a very competitive market. Our team was given a tight deadline of six weeks to complete the project."

Task: "My responsibility was to lead a cross-functional team consisting of members from marketing, design, engineering, and production. Our goal was to develop the product, create a marketing campaign, and ensure it was ready for launch within the specified time frame."

Action: "To address this challenge, I immediately called a team meeting to outline our strategy and set clear expectations. We broke down the project into smaller milestones and assigned specific tasks to each team member based on their expertise. I also established regular progress check-ins to monitor our timeline and identify any potential roadblocks. I also encouraged open communication and collaboration among team members, and when a design issue threatened to delay the project, I brought together the design and engineering teams to brainstorm solutions and we stayed on schedule."

Result: "Thanks to our efforts, we not only met the tight deadline, but also launched the product successfully. We received positive feedback from customers, and the product exceeded sales expectations in the first quarter, contributing significantly to our company's revenue."

Question 2: Can you tell me how, as a sales representative, you were able to increase revenue of your territory within the first year?

Situation: "In my previous role as a sales representative at ABC Corporation, I was assigned to a challenging territory with a history of stagnant sales and a declining customer base. The territory had been underperforming for several years, and the company was looking for a turnaround."

Task: "My primary task was to revitalize the sales performance in my territory, and increase revenue within the first year. I was given a specific revenue target of $500,000 in new sales to achieve, and it was clear that a strategic approach was necessary to achieve this goal." (Here is where you would name the beginning and ending revenue, i.e., "I grew the territory from $2.4 million to $3.1 million in annual sales.")

Action: "To address this challenge, I took several strategic actions: I conducted thorough market research and identified both potential opportunities and potential competition. I analyzed industry trends, revitalized product offerings, and gained insight into the needs of the businesses in my territory. I began building better relationships with existing clients, accounting for a $300,000 boost in sales of my products to existing clients, and the remaining growth I attributed to new account acquisition. I targeted businesses that aligned with our products and services. Through targeted cold calls, networking events, and attending industry trade shows, I generated a steady stream of qualified leads.

Result: "As a result of these strategic efforts, I successfully increased the revenue of my territory by $700,000 within the first year. This not only exceeded the revenue target set by the company, but also helped bring the territory back to a profitable status. I also had improved customer satisfaction scores and my efforts we recognized with a "Salesperson of the Year" award.

Question 3: As a medical office administrator, how did you improve patient satisfaction for your organization?

Situation: "In my role as a Medical Office Administrator at XYZ Healthcare Clinic, I inherited a situation where patient satisfaction had been steadily declining over the past year. The clinic had received several negative reviews, and patient feedback surveys consistently showed dissatisfaction with the overall patient experience."

Task: "My primary task was to identify the root causes of the declining patient satisfaction and implement changes to improve it. The organization recognized that patient satisfaction was crucial not only for patient well-being, but also for maintaining a positive reputation and retaining patients."

Action: "To address this challenge, I took the following actions: I started by thoroughly analyzing patient feedback and survey results to pinpoint specific pain points and areas where improvement was needed. This involved reviewing written feedback, conducting phone surveys, and analyzing online reviews.

Then I created very specific training tools for each of our staff members and addressed the importance of the patient experience. Instead of focusing on the negative feedback, I turned it around to reward our team based on positive patient experiences. I created contests, consistent feedback, and a team-driven approach to get our staff excited about positive reviews. They were competing with each other to deliver the BEST possible experiences, and everyone was sharing best practices with their peers.

I also developed some tools to reduce wait times, improved our scheduling systems, and improved patient communication regarding delays."

Result: "As a result of these actions, we witnessed a significant improvement in patient satisfaction for the organization. Our patient satisfaction scores increased by 25% over the course of a year, and negative reviews decreased significantly. Patients reported shorter wait times and improved communication with staff.

As a sidenote, employee morale also improved as staff felt more engaged and valued in contributing to the positive patient experience."

Now you are prepared to be a STAR! Every single person, every single job, every single experience has a story, and that story has an accomplishment, impact, or difference that you've made in your job or for your company. It is strange to think about ourselves in terms of actions, successes, and measurable results when we're just going to work every day, doing our jobs, and heading home. But if you want to be considered for higher level roles, that come with higher levels of pay, make sure you are documenting any accomplishments you've had, preferably while they are fresh in your mind. I recommend keeping an "active resume," which is a resume that you can send out when you see a job that strikes your fancy. I also recommend keeping a long-form resume, where you are weekly/monthly listing out work successes, accomplishments, impact, kudos, compliments, and recognitions as they happen. Some people have "long-form" resumes that number 20 or 30 pages, so when the time comes, and you need to write a resume or have a resume written to conduct a job search, all the juicy little nuggets of why you are awesome are contained in one place. It is a lot easier than trying to remember your successes from 10 years ago. Trust me, I know.

> There's a formula for everything, even interview questions.

24 | Job Hunting in a Terrible Job Market

I have a client who we began working with right at the outset of the Covid pandemic, an executive sales representative in the durable medical industry. She has been laid off or let go from her job three times since 2020. You heard that right: three times!

Is that just bad luck? Or a sign that something else was going on?

Well, since she's an amazing human, an amazing lady, and an amazing salesperson, I am going to say she has either been in the wrong place at the wrong time, or she has had some bad luck when it comes to her jobs.

The first layoff was because no one was having elective surgeries during the pandemic. She primarily sells products that are used in a surgical setting. Since they were not needed, her company RIF'd (reduction in force) half its team. She had only been there for 18 months, so low woman on the totem pole.

The second time she was laid off, it was because the company was struggling financially, and while she brought in a lot of revenue, the company decided to outsource its entire sales team of 30 people, and everyone lost their job.

The third time, she had taken a role quickly without really knowing what her job was going to be, and that was a mistake. When she started job No. 3, she found out she'd be covering eight states, was expected to travel five to six days a week, and was being paid 100% commissions on products that no one really wanted. When she complained about the lack of support, the lack of resources, and lack of opportunities, the company fired her.

All three times she signed up for unemployment benefits, all three times she ramped up for a job search.

During this time, she had sent out hundreds of resumes, interviewed with at least 25 different companies, and worked hard to maintain her positive attitude, composure, and outlook.

It was a tough time. A single mom of two little girls, she was scared, anxious, and exhausted. She thought about throwing in the towel and opening a consulting business, but didn't really have the safety net for that. At one point, she considered getting a part-time job to supplement her meager unemployment, but part-time jobs don't take kindly to multiple requests for days off to interview with other companies.

There was no doubt about it. She was beaten down, frustrated, and the nature of the interview process, lack of communication, and respect for her time was incredibly demoralizing.

Every single day she felt like she was beating her head against a wall. She was halfheartedly filing out application after application, taking calls from recruiters who never called her back or followed up, and was passed up for more jobs than you can imagine.

After her last opportunity fell through, she did something unexpected. She packed up her two kids and took them to the beach for two weeks. Yep, she took a vacation.

She needed to get away from her computer, her phone, her thoughts. She borrowed from her savings, planned a cost-conscious getaway, rented a condo for cheap, and spent two weeks playing with her daughters in the surf and making s'mores on the beach at night.

When she came home, she was reenergized, refocused, and determined to get herself on the right path.

She started off by calling, emailing, texting, and messaging anyone and everyone she knew. From friends, family, former co-workers, and old bosses to tell them she was looking for a job. She systematically made lists of companies she would be interested in working for.

She identified account executive roles in any industry she felt she could succeed in, and researched people on LinkedIn who she was connected to, asking for introductions at companies where they knew someone.

Within a few weeks, she had several interviews lined up, mostly by using a good resume and personal connections, and within a month, she landed a $130,000 job offer as an account executive in the wine and spirits industry.

She'd never sold these products before, but sales is sales is sales is sales, and as a good salesperson, she can sell anything. She changed industries, changed her outlook, changed her approach, and it worked out.

Don't be afraid to get out of your comfort zone. If you've always been a truck driver, there is no reason you cannot be a manager of the dispatch team. If you've always been in marketing, there is no reason why you cannot pivot into human resources or operations.

We are not just one thing; we are many things. We all have different experiences, we have different talents and skills, there is nothing you cannot learn, and there is nothing holding you back from being who you want to be professionally and living the life you want to live personally.

From my perspective there are three things you need to get a job in a tough market.

1. You must have a good resume and LinkedIn profile that does not pigeonhole you into one industry, one title, or one career. I see so many people who use their LinkedIn profile to promote their employers. Your LinkedIn profile is designed to promote YOU. And no one else.

2. You must be willing to reach out for help. That includes networking with your people, asking them to make introductions within companies that have a job you are interested in. Do not ask anyone to "keep your eyes open for a position for me"; instead, systematically, and specifically do the work, find out who knows whom, and use the LinkedIn job board to figure out who is connected at your target company.

3. You must be open-minded. Consider types of positions you've never held before but have the skills to do. No one ends up where they started out. A successful career is full of all kinds of twists and turns, all kinds of surprises, and all kinds of new and exciting adventures!

So, while a job search in a great market can be a challenge, looking for a new role in a terrible market can be a soul-sucking exercise in repetition, rejection, and frustration, don't despair. Terrible markets don't last forever. When the time is right for you to move on in your career, the only thing that really matters is your persistence, patience, and talent. And I know you have all three of those things.

> Suck it up buttercup: looking for a job in a bad market takes a dose of persistence, a sense of humor, and a little luck.

25

My Dad Never Made More Than $30,000 a Year

My dad never made more than $30,000 a year. He worked in a factory. Sometimes he bartended in the evenings or on the weekends. Sometimes he cut grass, took odd jobs, or did maintenance work. He never, ever, ever talked about money. Or being poor.

He is the happiest, smartest, kindest, funniest, and most competent human being I know, and have ever known. Now in his eighties, he is still the first person I call when something breaks or I need advice or I get the urge to take a spontaneous road trip.

He always says, "I'll be ready in 10 minutes."

Once he was working for an automotive manufacturer. He came up with this idea to repurpose a tool the company used, saving it millions of dollars a year. The company offered him a $10,000 bonus and a promotion into management. He took the $10,000 and turned down the promotion. He took us to Disney—the one and only elaborate vacation we ever took as a family.

Years later, I asked him why he turned down the promotion.

He told me "I loved getting home to your mother and you girls at 3 p.m. each day. I didn't want the headaches or time away from my family." Honestly, he was smart enough to be running the place . . . but he chose his life over his work.

Don't get caught up in the hype. So many posts, stories, or "advice" from people who say you can't be happy unless you make X amount of money. It's simply not true. I am fascinated by all the social media people who have adopted a simpler way of life. You know the ones: the homesteaders, the stay-at-home moms, the people who give up corporate jobs and buy a goat farm.

I've never been a big fan of cutting coupons, I am not great with a budget. This morning, I ordered 11 pairs of winter boots and came to realize when I got the confirmation email for my purchase that I already own one pair of the boots I'd just ordered. It's fine. I will give them to my daughter; we wear the same size. So, the idea of not having some play money to spend, or having to worry about how much my morning coffee is going to cost me, is not the way that I want to live. I know I'm not alone in that feeling.

I tell my kids, "There is nothing wrong with being poor, but there is nothing romantic about it either." I am certain that despite my ideal childhood that my parents had money worries; they just never really talked about it.

So, where is the work-life balance? Can we live with less? Do we want to? Those are only questions that you can answer, but I do know one thing . . . and that is that most people don't know what they are worth.

Yes, there are great companies out there that are dedicated to paying a fair wage, an honest paycheck, male/female salary equality, yada, yada, yada. But, on the other hand, there are plenty of employers who are trying to save a buck by making lowball job offers and hoping someone is desperate enough to take it.

How do you know if you are paid fairly?

There are tons of online resources where you can find great information about salaries, how your salary might compare to other salaries in the same field, the same industry, or the same geographical location.

Do your research and find out something called the "market value" for your position.

Say, for instance, you are a retail manager. In a rural area, you might make $65,000 a year. The cost of living might be lower; the groceries, rent, and essential costs are going to be cheaper in a small town in Idaho than they are in New York City.

Now, if you are a retail manager of a big box store, you are going to make $100,000, and that is consistent no matter where you live. Smaller companies may base salaries on the area, where larger companies are going to base salaries on the responsibilities of the store.

Throwing another wrench into the mix is "work from home (WFH)" versus "in office." For a while, WFH staff seemed to make less money, but now that so many companies have a fully remote staff, they had to even out salaries based on the job you are doing, and not where you are doing it from.

If you are an IT executive supporting a large company, its infrastructure, security, functionality, and so on, and managing a team, but you are doing it from Miami, Florida, you are probably going to make the same amount of money as your peer doing it from Des Moines, Iowa.

I am a huge believer in paying based on the job, not the job location. You don't work any fewer hours, you don't work less hard, you don't have fewer responsibilities. Companies are learning to adjust wages to retain talent, and taking into consideration cost-of-living expenses as they are making adjustments to their salary bands.

In summary, most people rely on their employers to tell them if they are being paid fairly, but I urge you to rely on yourself.

Ask yourself these questions:

1. Do I feel properly compensated for the work I am doing?
2. Are my peers, doing the same job, making more or less money than me?
3. If I am underpaid, what wage/salary would make me happy?

Ultimately, being paid, underpaid, overpaid, fairly paid, or anything else is all in your control. Not making enough money?

Do something else. Feel like you are working too hard, too many hours under too much stress for what you are making? Work less or take a less stressful job. At the end of the day, a job is a job is a job. Worry about your life, quality of life, and how you want to live first, then every decision you make about your career can follow that.

> True happiness combines wealth and intangibles: relationships, fulfillment, purpose.

26

From Cop to Millionaire

Many years ago, I received a phone call from a New York City police officer by the name of Tony. The reason for Tony's call? He was looking for resume services because he was going to try to transition from being a police officer into a new job.

Now Tony was not very happy about this transition. You see, Tony was a cop, his dad was a cop, so was his grandfather and two of his brothers, and countless uncles, cousins, and friends.

But on this day, during that phone call, he told me that his wife, the mother of his children, was begging him to be something, anything other than a police officer.

Tony had married his high school sweetheart, and together they had five beautiful children, all girls. When they married, he had just graduated from the police academy, so his wife knew that his passion was in law enforcement.

But as the years went by and their family grew, she became more and more anxious that "something would happen to him" and she would be left alone, raising five girls.

Nothing had happened; he had not been hurt at all, but his wife kept having dreams about him being hurt or killed. Now, I am no psychiatrist, and most would call this a rational fear, but to her, the dreams kept getting more and more real, and her anxiety was spilling from her nighttime life to her daytime life, and their arguments over his career were on the path to derailing their happy marriage.

So, when Tony called and he told me his story, I believed his efforts at getting a resume and applying for jobs was more of him going through the motions to appease his wife versus any real desire to stop being a police officer.

Tony and I hit it off right away. I am Italian; he is Italian. We talked about our kids, our lives, and our favorite dishes.

So, on that day, we began a friendship and business relationship that has since spanned over 17 years, 8 resume updates, holiday cards, and a career that went from New York City cop to $1-million-dollars-a-year head of security role with one of the biggest social media companies in the world. To this day, when he calls my office, he asks about my kids by their first names, and we connect and chat like we talked yesterday, instead of four or five years ago.

To be honest with you, I did not think that Tony was ever going to stop being a police officer. He loved it too much, and that showed in almost every interaction we had. But once his resume was completed, and he started taking it out for a spin, he was flabbergasted at the number of companies that were interested in a NYC cop with the right attitude, the right knowledge, and a penchant for making friends wherever he went.

I knew he was serious when, after landing his first interview, he called me to tell me that this potential new job was going to pay at least $10,000 more a year than his police officer salary, and for the first time, he was excited about where he could go. And keeping his wife happy was a bonus too!

How did Tony go from cop to executive? Well, first he went back to night school to finish his bachelor's degree in business. And with his shiny new resume and degree, he landed a job as a supervisor for a security company in New York City that liked to hire off-duty officers as security guards. His first few years were grueling, working the night shift, hiring, firing, training, supervising, and staffing guards at customer locations across the five boroughs.

After a few years, he got promoted to the head of operations, and then moved into a corporate security position with a global insurance company. It was there that he learned the ropes of corporate security: how to select the best technologies, resources, and vendors to ensure the safety and security of employees and visitors at the company's headquarters; how to identify potential threats; and he returned to school and earned his MBA.

He learned about access control systems, surveillance, and alarm systems. He built an entire department around travel and executive protection, including providing security for company VIPs as they traveled the world. In one hairy situation, he learned in real time how to hire and deploy an extraction team to rescue a high-level executive and his family from a foreign country when riots broke out and the U.S. Embassy came under siege. Part of being in this head of security role is to ensure the safety of key people within the organization, no matter where they might be.

From emergency response, crisis management, security compliance, budget management, and navigating complex international incidents, Tony really made a name for himself. In all of my dealings with him, he never changed his personality. He still talked like a cop, sounded like a cop, and above all, no matter how much money he made, his family, his wife, his (now plentiful) grandchildren were the center of his universe.

After not hearing from him for a few years, he called our office in a bit of a panic. He was tapped to interview for a head of global security job for a major media company with its headquarters in New York City. We did a quick resume update for him, and he sent it off. A few months later, he called to tell me he had just signed an employment agreement. I asked him, "What did they offer you?"

He laughed when he replied, "They offered me $1.2 million per year." I hooted and hollered, and we giggled like schoolgirls at the craziness of the turn his life had taken.

When I look back at the people I've met and their stories, I would say that this is one of my favorites. It is an amazing honor to be witness to such incredible career growth, and even more so, to be even a little part of helping someone get there.

> Choosing the path less traveled may be challenging, but it can lead to extraordinary destinations.

27

Is That Actually a Job?

I am endlessly fascinated by how people make a living. My new obsession is watching all these "homesteaders" online who give up the rat race, move to the country, grow their own food, and live off the land. They raise chickens, plant gardens, make bread from scratch, and head to Costco once a month with a $300 budget to get enough supplies to feed a family of six for a month.

As someone who DoorDashed $1,500 worth of dinners last month, I'd love to know how they do it.

Apparently, if you do it well enough, and enough people are interested in your story on social media, you can be paid through sponsorships. So, maybe, they are walking around in real life with designer purses and expensive sports cars, and putting on a show for you and me.

I have also been following a young couple who left their corporate jobs, bought an old school bus, turned it into their home away from home, and are traveling across the United States, documenting their trials and tribulations, and capturing it all on blogs, videos, and articles, and getting paid to do it.

Or, how about the people who quit their day jobs to become delivery drivers for all the delivery services that popped up during the Covid pandemic?

If you are struggling in your job, your boss is a nightmare, and your commute is a soul-sucking exercise in erratic drivers and road rage, giving it all up to go live among the trees, random wildlife, and homemade bread might sound pretty damn good right now.

But before you throw away your drug-store deodorant and the comforts of running water, electricity, and Wi-Fi, there are other options.

When I was growing up, you were either a full-time employee or you stayed home with your kids. I hardly knew anyone who worked a part-time job. There were some random moms who may have worked part-time at the mall or were substitute teachers, but for the most part, they either worked a 40-hour-a-week job or not.

But today, you have so many different options.

Now, there are part-time jobs, gig jobs, contract jobs, hybrid jobs, work-from-home jobs, flex jobs, seasonal jobs, and self-employment jobs.

So, how do you go from leaving a job you despise to one that you love?

Well, it's like I always say about driving in New York City. It's a scary thing, but the secret is to not be afraid of getting hit.

The challenge with most people who want to leave their jobs for greener pastures is money. They can't just up and walk away when they get into a fight with their boss, get taken advantage of, or really dislike the work they are doing. We all have bills to pay, and certain lifestyles that we've grown accustomed to, so we get caught up in the quagmire of going to work to get the paycheck to buy the things we want and need. You can't just stop paying your mortgage or eating . . . so we get caught in a never-ending game of catch-22.

Breaking the cycle of living the life you have versus the life you want can start at any time. Inevitably, there are sacrifices and you have to determine what you are willing to accept to get there.

When you are young, the sky is the limit. If you are not married, have no kids, and no major financial obligations, being able to take a chance on a nontraditional situation is within your grasp. As you get older, if you are married or have a significant other, bigger obligations, and can't just skip out on clothing and feeding your kids, it gets trickier.

The good news is that since we live in a global world, you don't have to limit your "dream job" search to your local area. Since so many positions are remote nowadays, you can find your passion with a company that is located nowhere near you. If you love art, have always dreamed of living in Paris, there is nothing stopping you from applying to a social media manager position at the Louvre, even if you live in Paris, Kentucky, instead of Paris, France.

Or if you love food, you can be a food stylist, food photographer, or food critic from anywhere. The key is to find publications, outlets, and employers that share your passion, have found a way to commoditize the job, and razzle dazzle them with your resume and ability to contribute your skills and knowledge.

I once worked with a client who was employed in the technology industry as a sales executive, and he grew to hate it over the years. But he had two kids, a big mortgage, and a wife who wanted to maintain their expensive lifestyle, so he felt trapped.

As we interviewed him to develop his resume, he told us he loved and lived for the weekends. Both of his boys were amateur motor cross racers, and each weekend, he'd load up their bikes and travel all over the region so they could compete in races.

I suggested to him that since he was in sales, he could basically sell anything, and if he was tired of technology, he should explore opportunities he was interested in, like motor cross. He kind of chuckled at the idea, and said, "So you think I should go sell motorcycles?"

"Well," I told him, "yes and no. I am not suggesting that you go to the local retailer and ask for a job selling bikes, but you should check out all the biggest bike manufacturers in the world and see if they are hiring in any executive roles."

Six months later, he accepted an offer to be the head of U.S. sales and distribution for one of the largest motorcycle manufacturers in Europe. He figured out a way to leverage his love of sales, his passion for racing, and STILL keep his family well supported.

Ultimately, there are tons of different kinds of jobs, work situations, and ways to make a living. You don't have to settle for one thing or another. You can be around people who excite you, in an industry you are interested in, and work at a job that fits your life, not the other way around.

> When you work at a job you love, you'll never work a day in your life.

28 | Are You Underpaid?

Going to work each day, feeling undervalued, underappreciated, and unfulfilled is not a good feeling. For many people, being underpaid is common, even accepted. But if you are at the point where you no longer wish to just keep the status quo, you must ask yourself, "Am I underpaid and how do I know for sure?"

Well, first you must know the answer to this question: "Do I feel justly compensated for the time, effort, expertise, and work I am doing?"

Second, you need to see what the going rate for your job is. Tools like salary.com, payscale.com, Glassdoor, SalaryExpert, and others can give you that information. The U.S. Bureau of Labor Statistics has tools as well. Another way is to search for your job, job title, size of company, and location on places like LinkedIn or Monster.com and see if the salaries that are being shown for similar jobs are, in fact, similar to what you are making.

I believe in gut instinct, as well as how you feel about your job, the amount of work you are doing, and how valued you feel. So while these guides and resources can help you to figure out if you are being paid fairly, I think you probably already know if you are or you are not.

There is a lot of talk about how some people must work a full-time job and a gig/side hustle to make ends meet. While I applaud anyone who does that, most full-time jobs should be enough to take care of your expenses. If it is not, you either need to look at your expenses (tough, I know) or look at your salary. If you cannot work one job, pay your rent, feed yourself, cover your student loans, and have a little bit of fun money left, you probably need to change jobs or change your lifestyle.

There is nothing wrong with a little financial struggle; it builds character; helps you to determine how to best budget your resources; and allows you to learn one of life's hardest lessons, which is that you cannot have everything you want all the time. But a struggle shouldn't last for more than a few years of your professional career, and if it does, you may have to think really hard about what you want your life to look like.

We do a lot of resume packages for people in sales. I am not talking about 100% commission sales or insurance sales or door-to-door sales. I am referring to account executives, business development representatives, regional sales executives, and so on. These are all titles that basically mean that while you are selling a product or service, you have a base salary, a compensation or commission structure, and either a group of named accounts or some targeted group of customers you are selling to.

It is one of the most common jobs in the world, and every kind of company, from technology to healthcare to resume services, has people doing the jobs of sales. For the most part, your comp will be based on how much, in real dollars, you are selling. If you work for IBM or Google or Microsoft, you will likely make over $100,000 annually plus a bonus or commission. Why? Those are companies that a lot of customers do business with, and their products are tried and true, meaning that everyone knows who they are and most business customers are going to have a need for the technologies they create.

Their account executives are typically given a group of accounts or a territory that they are going to call on to educate their customers, close sales, farm for new opportunities within an account, or manage their current business. This is more what we refer to as account management. They are great jobs if you like sales, meeting new customers, hitting your sales goals, and winning new business. I've had clients in sales make $50,000 a year, and I've had clients in sales that make well over $1 million a year. To me, it seems that the people we work with that make the MOST money are almost always in a sales role.

Years ago, we did two resumes for two sales representatives who were selling "financial industry research" tools. Their products were basically a set of quantitative and qualitative research tools that money managers use to make considerations and decisions about what or where to invest their money. These products are sold to your Wall Street types, hedge fund managers, venture capitalists (VCs), and other investors.

We worked with them both within a week or two of each other. One of our clients was working out of New York City. His salary was around $200,000 a year plus commission. The other client was working out of the Pacific Northwest. His salary was $400,000 a year plus commission.

They were both selling nearly the exact same products to almost all the same people. So why was one making nearly $200,000 more than the other?

Here's why. The guy working for the company based in New York City was a well-established company. It was well known in the industry, had all the big financial firms on its roster, and those customers were going to continue to buy those products regardless. So, his job was to wine and dine them, ask them what they needed, take his biggest customers golfing, and make sure they were happy. It was not a difficult job for him as he knew the products, knew the people, and had longevity in his role.

The guy out of the Pacific Northwest was working for a company that had spent tons of time, effort, resources, and funding to build out their products, which were much more advanced. Early on, the company had no dedicated sales team to speak of. So, my client had to go and build relationships, establish a customer base, explain to everyone what these products did, why they were better, and how the customer could leverage it to make more money for its customers.

So, same/similar product, but very different salary and commission structures.

When you think you're underpaid, how do you verify it? You do the work, you do the research, and you check all the websites and resources. You now have verified that you are being underpaid. What do you do?

In my experience, there are three effective ways to negotiate a raise.

1. Threat

Imagine what you might do if you found out you were being paid nearly $75,000 less than your male peers for doing the same job. That is exactly what happened to a client of ours, an associate at a law firm, when someone from HR mistakenly (accidentally or on purpose) forwarded the associates salary report to her.

She had been with the firm for nearly six years, and twice received a nominal 4% raise. So, imagine her surprise when an email showed up in her inbox with a spreadsheet attached with all the salaries of the 60 associates employed by the firm. She was a third-year associate, and the only female. When she looked down through the list, she quickly recognized that her third-year associate peers, all men, were making between $200,000 and $215,000, and she was making $125,000.

Of course, her first inclination was to march right into her boss's office (right after she cried in the bathroom) and demand to be paid fairly. But she did not do that. She left early that day, went home, and formulated a plan. She realized that if the information was sent to her on purpose, it was because someone in HR wanted her to know. She had never received an inadvertent email during her time there, and she was sure she was not receiving one now. But, she also did not know if she could use this spreadsheet to make her case, and she certainly did not want to get anyone in trouble.

So, after thinking long and hard, consulting some friends, and her dad (also an attorney), she decided to send her boss an email instead of asking for a meeting. She wasn't scared to ask for a meeting, but she wanted to give her boss an easy way out before having a blowup.

She crafted a short note:

"I hope this email finds you well. I wanted to discuss an important matter regarding my current compensation. Recently, I became aware that my salary is significantly lower compared to my peers in similar roles within the organization. According to my research, there is a notable discrepancy of $75,000 between their salaries and mine.

I am sure that this is a clerical or administrative oversight, as I am certain that my being the only female third-year associate on the team could not possibly be the reason that I am being paid less than my male counterparts.

At this time, I request an immediate rectification of this error, along with any relevant retroactive pay that I may be qualified for, and we can move on from this error.

If I do not see an increase in my compensation moving forward, I will assume that the decision to pay me less than my male counterparts was a conscious one, and I will, in turn, be forced to make my current situation known at another level within the organization.

Thank you for your time and attention to this matter. And as always, I remain a dedicated, loyal, and contributing member of your team."

Her boss answered her with a curt "this has been taken care of" email, and six months later she quit after landing another job.

While this situation (if it were me) would have been dealt with by me storming into the boss's office and demanding to know why I wasn't being paid the same as my male counterparts, she did all the right things. She remained calm. She thought about what she wanted to say without rocking the boat, she was professional, she crafted her approach carefully, and it worked in her favor. It also allowed her to be paid on par with her male peers as she looked for another job. Ultimately, she knew she would not be staying on after what she'd found out, but her cool head and professional approach gave her the time she needed to plan her exit.

What should you do if you ever find yourself in a similar situation?

First, take a deep breath. While it is incredibly frustrating and disappointing to know that you are making less, or WAY less, than your peers, there could be several reasons why.

You may have less experience, you may live in a region where the cost of living is lower than others, or you could be in a situation where salary disparity is the norm.

Of these three things, only the third is illegal. Being paid less money because you are a female versus male is illegal in the United States.

The Equal Pay Act requires that men and women in the same workplace be given equal pay for equal work.

After you've uncovered the disparity, reach out to your HR contact. Let them know that you've recently found out that your pay is not on par or equal to your male counterparts. Give them the chance to make the correction or explain why that might be. In many cases, the wage gap might be unintentional. Share your evidence and ask for an explanation of the pay disparity.

Know Your Rights: Familiarize yourself with the relevant laws and regulations in your jurisdiction that prohibit gender-based wage discrimination. This might include federal, state, or local laws as well as company policies.

Request a Salary Review: Ask for a formal salary review to evaluate whether your compensation aligns with your qualifications, experience, and the company's pay practices. During the review, make sure to highlight your achievements and contributions to the company.

Seek Legal Advice: If discussions with your employer do not yield satisfactory results, consult an attorney or legal expert experienced in employment discrimination cases. They can help you understand your legal rights and options.

File a Complaint: If you believe you are experiencing wage discrimination due to your gender, you may file a complaint with relevant government agencies, such as the Equal Employment Opportunity Commission (EEOC) in the United States. They can investigate your case and take appropriate action.

Document Everything: Throughout the process, keep detailed records of all communications, meetings, and actions related to your wage discrimination complaint. This documentation can be crucial if you need to pursue legal action.

2. Persuasion

You've been working hard, working overtime, doing the work of several people, making your goals, and showing enthusiasm for your work. But at your most recent annual review, you were not acknowledged, appreciated, or praised in any way for your dedication. You received either no raise, or a small one. Now, the problem with getting no raise or a small raise is that your boss will usually blame this on a budgeting problem. "There is no money allocated for additional raises," or, "The powers-that-be have determined that this year, we are doing standard raises across the board." I have found this to be a common excuse, and by all accounts, it could be true. So, make sure when you approach your boss that you are doing so in a way that communicates not only why you deserve a raise, but also how much more it would cost to replace you.

The fact of the matter is that most people who deserve a raise don't always get one, and your employer relies on the fact that you will take what you are given. But, when you are a valuable employee for the company, they will almost always reconsider when they think they might lose you. It is common knowledge that pay raises do not always keep up with market value for your position. It is nearly 100% accurate that replacing you will cost them more, sometimes much more, than what a raise would cost to keep you.

First, you need to prepare your case: Start by thoroughly evaluating your contributions, achievements, and responsibilities within the organization. Make a list of your accomplishments, both quantitative (e.g., meeting sales targets, cost savings) and qualitative (e.g., leadership, problem-solving).

Gather Evidence: Collect the details of your performance, such as positive feedback from clients, colleagues, or supervisors, and awards or certifications.

Timing: Schedule a meeting with your boss—not on a Monday or a Friday, and do it after lunch. Never ask for a raise during a period of financial strain, during quarterly business results, or annual budget planning meetings. Never ask for a raise during a PR crisis or negative business event.

Craft Your Pitch: Be enthusiastic, start off by talking about how much you like your job and enjoy working there. Emphasize how your contributions have positively impacted the company, including increased revenue, improved processes, or enhanced team dynamics. Present your research on industry standards to demonstrate that your request is based on market conditions and commensurate titles/positions. Highlight any additional work or responsibilities you've recently taken on, and any additional hours you've worked.

Practice Your Presentation: Make sure to rehearse your speech. Ask a friend or partner to listen to your presentation and provide constructive feedback. Asking for a raise doesn't work if you are stumbling, mumbling, or outwardly nervous. Always make direct eye contact. The more confident you are in WHY you deserve a raise, the more likely your boss will be on your side. Quickly address any potential objections, and while you don't want to issue ultimatums—this is about persuasion, not threats—make it known that you know and understand your value. Make it clear that your request for a raise reflects your desire to grow within the organization, not just your desire for more money.

Make a Reasonable Suggestion: You want to present your boss with a number, so make sure that you have one in mind. You may not get your full request, so be open to an interim compromise. If your boss needs time to consider your request, ask for a specific timeline for a decision, and follow up as agreed.

If you do not receive a raise and believe you are not being compensated fairly, you should look at all your options, including seeking employment with other organizations or applying for internal promotions that more closely align with your salary expectations.

3. **Quit**

I know! This sounds like a very extreme way to get a raise. But 90% of the time it works. But it is not actually a "raise" per se; it is typically referred to as a counteroffer strategy, and here is how it works.

If you've gone through the proper channels, asked for a raise, presented your case, and have diligently performed your work, met your goals, and gained recognition for your work, but you are still underpaid, you may need to consider looking for a new job.

Oftentimes, going after a new job is a knee-jerk reaction when you are frustrated with your current role, for all the reasons I've mentioned. You like your job, you like your co-workers, and for the most part, you like your employer, but feel as though your efforts are not being rewarded and that can prompt what we like to call "the counteroffer strategy."

This is when you actively apply for a new position, and plan to use that new offer to gain leverage with your current employer, forcing their hand to vocalize their commitment to your employment in the form of a raise or a promotion (with a raise to go along). In other words, you are forcing their hand.

I've seen this approach work, but I've also seen it backfire. Either way, it is a risky proposition. So, you must first ask yourself, "Am I prepared to live with the consequences?"

If the answer is "yes," then this might be the approach for you.

The first thing you want to do is assess your reasons for wanting a raise and whether quitting is the right solution.

Are you genuinely unhappy with your current job or is the primary motivator a higher salary?

Second, you will want to secure a new job offer: Start by looking for a new job and actively interviewing with other companies. Keep in mind that not all interview/offer processes are short and sweet. You must be committed to a lengthy interview process, interviewing with multiple companies, multiple times, and there may be travel, interview assignments, personality assessments, skills tests, and reference checks involved. Make sure to approach this search under the assumption that you are not only doing this to get a counteroffer from your current employer, but may actually consider taking a new job if a good offer is presented to you. Ensure that you are pursuing roles that come with a significantly higher salary or better overall compensation package than your current position.

Third, you've landed an offer from another organization. Now what? Once you've received a written job offer from a new employer, inform your current employer of your intention to resign. Be professional and respectful in your resignation letter and during the conversation.

Fourth, anticipate a counteroffer: It's possible that your current employer may try to retain you by offering a counteroffer, which could include a salary increase, improved benefits, or other incentives. Should you take it? Evaluate the offer. Is it enough to make you reconsider leaving? In addition to the salary increase, has the company made any adjustments to your working conditions? Benefits? Promotional opportunities? In other words, how far are they willing to go to keep you? Does it solve all the issues you have with your current situation?

In my opinion, if you are leveraging a new job offer to get what you want, take the counteroffer. But, if you started looking for a new position because you were unhappy in your original job, don't take the counteroffer. More money does not solve the problem of being unhappy in your job.

So the final advice I have for you is this. If you only started looking for a new position because of the salary you were making, it is smart to leverage a new job offer to get what you want. Once you've made your choice, commit to it wholeheartedly. Continue to perform well in your current role and strive to make the most of the opportunities available to you.

But, if you don't like your job, are unhappy in your day-to-day work, or you've been feeling restless, unchallenged, or underappreciated, those things will not go away with more money. Those things will only go away when you find yourself in a position that makes you happy and fulfilled.

> The very best advocate you'll ever have for you . . . is YOU!

29 | Fired? Welcome to the Club.

At one time in every professional's life, the likelihood of getting fired is pretty good. It is said that 40% of people are fired from at least one job in their lifetime, and I think that number is an underestimate. Most people, when faced with the prospect of "getting fired" or "resigning," will choose to resign, so the statistics are markedly lower.

During the Covid pandemic, 18 million people in the United States were laid off, and in 2022, 15.4 million people lost their jobs. That is a lot of people looking for new jobs, moving between jobs, deciding to never go back to work, starting businesses, and entering the gig economy.

From major corporations to small businesses, no one was immune to the job losses during the pandemic, and some industries like hospitality, restaurants, amusement parks, movies and movie theaters, and casinos were gutted. As the pandemic passed, and the economy began to return, the next phase of layoffs occurred in 2022 and 2023, hitting the tech, banking, finance, and retail sectors.

The reason I am sharing this is to show you that layoffs do not discriminate. They can happen to any person, any company, any sector, and any industry at any time. So, based on these numbers, and my assumptions, there is at least a 50% chance of you getting laid off in your career.

How should you handle it? Well, it's not like those TikTok videos where people tell their bosses off and quit their jobs, which are highly amusing, but definitely not recommended. Nor is it as dramatic as getting called into the office, having a go-round with HR or your boss, and then leaving in tears. For the most part, it's not done with great fanfare or drama, even though you have been caught off-guard, blindsided, and surprised that your loyalty to the company has resulted in your termination.

Today, most terminations or firings are done digitally. You get locked out of the company systems in the middle of the night and wake to an email (to your personal email address) letting you know that you've been let go. Or you are asked to join a Zoom meeting during which the CEO of your company tells the 200 or 2000 people on the call that you are all being laid off.

Do you remember the digital mortgage company Better CEO doing a mass layoff of 900 people over Zoom? The call, which was recorded by one of those employees and posted online, was three minutes long and delivered completely void of expression or empathy. Better's second-round of layoffs made news when severance payments were prematurely deposited into the bank accounts of staff who had not yet learned they were losing their jobs.

Some layoffs are predictable, and some are quite unexpected. Here is how to be prepared for both.

There are six very specific signs that you are about to get laid off. These layoffs happen because of a performance problem (company or personal), a culture problem, or a "boss" problem.

Company Financial Troubles: If your company is facing financial difficulties, such as declining revenue, missed earnings targets, or frequent cost-cutting measures, it may increase the likelihood of layoffs. If your expense report can't get approved or someone starts questioning your lunch bills, mileage reimbursements, or you've been told that you cannot spend money on a new program, initiative, or project, those are red flags.

Reduced Workload: If you see a significant reduction in your workload or your department is not very busy, that can be a sign that your role is being phased out or that your department is downsizing. If a handful of people are let go or your boss is fired, you probably will be too.

Management Changes: If the company had four CEOs in the past two years or your leadership team looks like a revolving door, that could indicate trouble and a forthcoming restructuring, which may include layoffs. If you hear about private equity, investor visits, or heaven forbid, a merger or acquisition, your job could be made redundant. That means that basically when a company merges or acquires another company, there are two (or more) of you doing the same job. Most companies only need one CEO, COO, CFO, Head of Accounting, Head of Marketing, and so on. You get the picture.

Gossip: This is probably the one time you should pay attention to rumors and office gossip. If you start hearing rumors about impending layoffs or see colleagues leaving unexpectedly, it might be a sign that the company is planning reductions.

Unexpected Performance Reviews or Performance Improvement Plans: If you all of a sudden start receiving negative feedback on your previously stellar work, that is a red flag. If you cannot please your boss no matter how you try, red flag. If you are summoned into HR or a meeting with your boss and put on a PIP (Performance Improvement Plan), the writing is on the wall. A termination is forthcoming. I don't really know why companies go through the song and dance of this approach. We live in an "at will" employment environment; you can be let go at any time, for any reason, but a lot of companies like to cover their butts and document their actions to let you go, just in case you get a lawyer and try to cause a row.

Cuts in Benefits or Perks: If your company cuts your health insurance benefits, signs you up for a cheaper plan, reduces its retirement or 401(k) contributions, bonuses, or your home internet reimbursements, you are probably getting laid off soon. Not always, of course. Many companies facing financial difficulties WILL try to reduce costs to keep their staff, but this does not always work and people, for the most part, are the most expensive expense on the books.

For unexpected layoffs, there may be no real red flags, no warning shots, no gossip, or premonition. Sometimes companies make decisions to leverage sweeping layoffs to save tons of money, capitulate to investors, or circumvent potential industry or sector slowdowns. Even though you may be let go through no fault of your own, there are ways to prepare to move on.

Here are my top seven tips for every employee in preparing for a potential layoff.

1. **Keep Copies of All Your Performance Reviews and Employment Records.** Won an award? Take a photo of it, keep the certificate, and start a career "brag book" that showcases any honors, awards, recognitions, contests, or kudos you've received during your career. Trust me, you will thank me later. Do you have any idea how hard it is to try to remember your sales quota or employee of the year award 20 years from now when you are updating your resume? I do.

2. **Update Your Resume and LinkedIn Profile:** Always keep your resume and LinkedIn profile up to date with your latest accomplishments and skills. Take a few moments a few times a year to keep your information current. Finish a project? Add the details. Get a promotion, note the reasons why on your resume. Receive some type of recognition? Capture it. This will make it easier to start a job search if necessary. It doesn't matter if you have 30 pages of notes over the course of your career, it can all be easily condensed and turned into a resume.

3. **Save Money:** As someone with a shoe obsession and a spending problem, I feel like a bit of hypocrite telling you to save some money, but . . . save some money. It is important that you have a minimum of six months' worth of living expenses at the ready, just in case you lose your job. Those expenses should include your rent/mortgage, health insurance payment (you will be eligible to COBRA your benefits, but you must pay each month after losing your job), groceries, car payment, entertainment,

utilities, and so on. If you don't already have a personal budget, make one so you're know the actual numbers and plan your savings safety net to accommodate what you need.

4. **Job Search and Networking:** I always say that the best time to look for a job is always. You should always be on the lookout for new and better positions, even if you are still employed, even if you're happy in your position. It is best to build your network, make new business friends, develop relationships with recruiters, all while you are still working. If a layoff happens, you at least have a group of people and professionals willing to say a kind word, give you a reference, or make an introduction.

5. **Collect Recommendations:** During your career, you should always have people write you recommendations. Starting from your favorite professor in high school or college and moving to your peers, a boss who loved you, or customers whom you do business with, a short recommendation on your LinkedIn profile has been the key to winning an interview more times than I can count. When a third party says something nice about you, it is often more important than anything you can say about yourself. Don't be shy in asking for them; they come in really handy in a job search.

6. **Talk to HR:** While HR is employed by the company, it can also be an ally to the employees of that company. You can go to HR for many reasons, including career planning, to file a complaint, to get directions on how to best use your benefits or optimize your 401(k) contributions. The department should be a resource for you for all things related to your work, including a potential layoff. If you have concerns about the stability of your job, you've heard rumors of potential layoffs, or you just need to talk to someone "in the know," HR can be your friend. So, if you feel like something is amiss or that a layoff may be in your future, make an appointment with your HR department. You may be surprised to get a straight, honest answer, but ultimately, if you've been friendly with HR

in the past, you may have built enough trust to find out what is really going on.

7. **Legal Advice:** When you are being laid off, you will be presented with information about your severance package, health insurance benefit continuation, and a bevy of other documents, agreements, and legally binding paperwork. Do not sign anything in the heat of the moment. Companies have been known to back door noncompete clauses, NDAs, and other slimy or shady agreements into a severance packages, catching you off-guard and taking advantage of the delicate nature of the situation. When you are presented with this package, tell them you will take it with you and then take it to a lawyer. Now, if you are a college student working in a fast-food restaurant, ignore this advice. Sign up for unemployment benefits, and go study or go to a party. But if you are a salaried employee with skin in the game, make sure you are making the most of your severance and benefits packages. Consult your employee agreement to ensure you are being offered the standard or better package; do not agree to any type of clause like a noncompete on nondisparagement agreement, and companies cannot withhold your severance package for refusing to sign one. Sometimes, when you are being laid off, you may also be getting screwed. Talking to an employment or labor attorney will help you make the most of this situation.

There is a great line in one of my all-time favorite movies, *An American President*: "The secret to not panicking, is to actually NOT be panicking."

While losing a job can be an incredibly challenging and emotional experience, the more prepared you are to lose it, the better off you are. That is why it is so important to never think of any job as permanent.

As a side note, since so many people are losing their jobs and getting caught up in layoffs and workforce reductions, here are some things you can do to help a friend, family member, or peer when their job goes away.

- Start by acknowledging their emotions and letting them know that it's okay to feel upset, anxious, or frustrated. Say something like, "I can imagine this is really tough for you right now, and it's completely normal to feel this way."
- Be a compassionate and nonjudgmental listener. No need to give advice at this time. Encourage them to share their thoughts and feelings and resist the urge to try to solve the issue (you can't). Sometimes the best thing you can do is to let them vent.
- If you can, offer assistance with practical matters, such as updating their resume, searching for job openings, or reviewing financial options. This can alleviate some of the stress associated with job loss. Always be willing to make introductions if you know someone who is hiring, and encourage them to really think about what makes sense for them in their next career move.
- Take them to dinner, out to lunch, or invite them over for some fun. Emphasize the importance of self-care and engage them in activities to manage stress or take their minds off things.

My favorite thing to do when we get a call from someone who lost their job is to commiserate. Let them talk about how awful it was. Let them talk about how angry they are and agree they are right to feel that way. But this is also a golden opportunity to let someone know that maybe they were underemployed, or this situation might be a blessing in disguise, as it can be a stepping-stone or the nudge they needed to explore a new path. There is nothing better than empowering someone who is feeling down!

> No job is ever permanent. Always be on the lookout for something new.

30

Hiring Is a Hot Mess

An executive client of ours, a CEO of a tech startup, was interviewing for a new job after his old company had been sold. He was and is an amazing guy, a solid leader, and a hustler. He was originally brought into the tech startup, which was creating an app for the restaurant reservation industry, to lead strategy, organizational development, and commoditization of its portfolio of products. When he arrived there, the company was 100% funded by a handful of investors. When he left there, the business was sold to a MUCH bigger fish for over $15 million.

During his six years with that company, he learned everything you would need to know to run a small tech startup. From hiring the right people to managing the budgets to winning the hearts and minds of investors to building a solid engineering team, he had done it all.

When the time came and his CEO contract ended post-acquisition, he took a few months off to enjoy some time with his wife and two elementary school-aged children.

After taking some long overdue family vacations, getting to know his wife again (after regularly working 80-hour weeks), he dove back into the job search pool. He was referred to our company by a friend of his, and we created his resume, LinkedIn profile, and bio for a job search.

He started landing interviews almost immediately and was entertaining some pretty good offers. But unfortunately, they were all with similarly sized startups with all the same problems he'd faced in his previous role. No money, lack of direction, and 80-hour work weeks.

Because he wanted to spend time with his children before they went to college (they were 7 and 10), he decided he would rather pursue a role with an already established company. Most executives are resigned to the fact that they will work more than the standard 40 hours a week, and he was fine with that, but he did not want to sign on to another startup.

So, he began applying for VP of operations and CEO roles for smallish tech organizations. He landed an interview with a 10-year-old company that was fully staffed, had a good foothold in providing software solutions for the hospitality industry, and an operations budget that had been profitable for the past four years.

During his first interview, he chatted about his background, got into some details about the issues this company had, which were mostly growth related, and how he could leverage his knowledge and experience to get them into serious growth mode. That interview was with the HR director.

His second interview was with the Chief Operating Officer. During that interview, the COO discussed the dynamics of the team, the company's lack of training and development programs, as well as some diversity and inclusion programs the company wanted him to champion.

In his third and fourth interviews, senior leadership talked specifics about the market, potential new channels where the company could promote its software, as well as some sales initiatives the company wanted him to get involved in.

This went on for four more interviews.

At that point, he had said everything he could say. He met with some of the company's staff, attended a networking event with the COO, went to a sales meeting with its VP of Business Development, and waited for an offer.

Senior leadership asked him and his wife to a dinner, where the COO, VP of HR, CMO and a few other leaders would be in attendance. They went, had a great time, everyone seemed to get along, and he was sure an offer was forthcoming.

He waited a week, then another, then another. One month after the dinner, he finally got an offer, which he accepted. It was a nice bump in pay, around $60,000 more than he had been making, but it was closer to home, and he was feeling good about the balance he was going to have.

The entire process took nearly four months.

So here is the kicker. His wife was a dean of students for a small college on the West Coast. Six months after he started his new job, she received an out of the blue offer to be the dean of students at a much larger college on the East Coast. After lots of discussion, some tears, and several visits to the East Coast college, as a family, they decided she would accept the offer.

No matter how many times you interview someone, no matter how many dinners, discussions, or hoops you have people jump through, it doesn't mean they will stay in the role.

Not all interviews go this way, but if you are an executive, don't expect to get an offer after one or two touches.

Most interview processes at this level can go on for weeks or months. We see an average of three to four months of interviewing for ONE job before an offer is made for anyone with an executive level title.

As someone who is a big, big fan of instant gratification, and aren't we all, this can seem like a daunting process. But when you are after a big paycheck, expect to see a big interview timeline. Here is an example of some of the things you can be facing when interviewing for an executive level role.

Application and Resume Review:

The initial stage involves HR or a recruitment team reviewing applications and resumes to shortlist candidates who meet the basic qualifications and experience required for the executive role. This is where your resume may be plucked out of a proverbial pile of applicants, or when your resume has enough keywords to ping the applicant tracking system (ATS), and score your application as "qualified."

Screening Interview:

In this stage, a recruiter or HR professional conducts an initial phone or video interview to gauge the candidate's interest, availability, and to get a sense of their personality and communication skills. Some of these screenings may feel a bit disjointed, as the person conducting them tends to be a lower-level HR professional, or what I like to call a screener. The questions may be more general in nature, and are the same questions they are asking the top 8 or 10 candidates.

HR Interview:

Once you've passed the telephone prescreen, a more in-depth interview with an HR representative or recruiter during which the candidate's career history, motivations, and cultural fit with the company are assessed. Salary expectations and other administrative matters may also be discussed. It is at this time that I recommend that you get at least the salary range for the position. If the range is not aligned with your salary history or goals, it is best to bow out now before getting into the more intensive part of the process. If the salary range aligns with your expectations, carry on.

Initial Interview with the Hiring Manager:

The candidate meets with the hiring manager, often the executive they will report to. This interview focuses on the candidate's qualifications, relevant experience, and alignment with the organization's goals and culture. This is where you should be prepared with your STAR answers (see Chapter 23), and able to give specific examples of how your experience, skills, and accomplishments fit what they are looking for in this role. It is a great idea to ask questions about the challenges of this job and what problems, obstacles, or opportunities they are hoping to solve or gain.

Panel Interview:

A panel interview involves multiple senior-level employees or stakeholders who evaluate the candidate's leadership, decision-making abilities, and overall fit for the role. Questions may cover strategic vision and problem-solving skills. This is my least favorite part of the process. Panel interviews can seem unnerving. Either by design or happenstance, when four or five people are asking different questions, it can feel a bit chaotic and disjointed. Keep your cool, try to stay on task, and recognize that part of this process is really designed to see how you perform under pressure.

Technical or Functional Interview:

For executive roles with a strong technical or functional component, candidates may undergo an interview with experts in that domain to assess their competence and expertise. You may also be asked to take assessments to gauge your level of knowledge of a certain topic. For instance, if you are an executive in compliance in the healthcare industry, they may administer a test to see if you can explain, work through, and identify the most common vernacular or terminology as it applies to this role.

Behavioral Interviews:

These interviews delve into the candidate's past behavior, focusing on specific examples of leadership, teamwork, conflict resolution, and other soft skills that are vital for an executive position. This is where you are going to have your answers armed and ready to go. Questions may involve things like "Tell me about a time you took an underperforming team and turned them around" or "How would you handle a situation with a customer who wants to break our relationship or agreement?"

Case Study or Presentation:

Candidates may be asked to analyze a business case, develop a strategic plan, or deliver a presentation on a topic relevant to the position, demonstrating their decision-making and problem-solving abilities. I have extremely mixed feelings about asking candidates to provide nonpaid consulting work, which is exactly what these requests are. I've had clients who've spent weeks developing business plans, sales plans, budget and board presentations that were incredibly intensive, only to come to find that the company hired no one for the role and took their ideas and ran with them. While you might think this is highly unethical (and it is), there is nothing illegal about this practice. My advice is to never agree to do a presentation or case study that takes more than a few hours of your time, and never, ever leave a copy behind. You can present it on a PowerPoint, watermark it, then take it with you.

Stakeholder Interviews:

Candidates may meet with key stakeholders, such as board members, investors, or partners, to assess how they would interact with external constituents and whether they can build and maintain critical relationships. These can be fun experiences, involve going to a dinner or event, and getting to know the key decision-makers in the organization. If you've gotten to this point, you are one of the last two or three candidates they are considering.

Final Interview with Senior Leadership:

This interview typically involves meeting with the top executives or C-suite members. It may focus on the candidate's long-term strategic vision, alignment with the company's mission, and their potential contribution to the organization's success. If you've arrived at this interview, you are one of the last two remaining candidates.

After thoroughly reviewing credentials, interview performance, and coming to a consensus on their top candidate, the organization may conduct reference checks, verify your education, and contact previous employers to confirm your employment and salary history. Once that is completed satisfactorily, an offer will be made.

Go you!

> Interviews can be long and laborious, or short and sweet. Find out what you are getting into before you say "yes!"

31

Toxic Bosses

Our phone rings all day long with potential clients who need resume services so they can begin the process of conducting an effective job search.

We always ask them about their situation, whether they are employed currently or unemployed. We ask why they are looking for a new role, what type of position they'd like to go after, and what sort of salary range they are targeting.

Inevitably, we hear stories about terrible jobs, terrible situations, terrible pay, or lack of forward growth in their careers. There are many things that make people want to leave where they are and head somewhere else, but over the past few years "toxic boss" is rearing its ugly head and is a main reason why someone wants to move on.

As the pressure to keep businesses profitable amid challenging economic environments, the shit, as they say, rolls downhill. Your boss may be under extreme pressure to do more with less, or have the higher-ups within the company demanding that business return to pre-pandemic levels of service, profitability, and growth. This can be a stressful situation for anyone, even the most experienced or seasoned professionals. It is certainly not an excuse for poor behavior, but it may explain why "toxic boss" cases are on the rise.

So, what is a *toxic boss*? Basically, it's a manager or supervisor who exhibits harmful and detrimental behavior in the workplace. Through their words, actions, and attitudes, they can create a hostile and unhealthy work environment for anyone who is reporting to them.

Toxic bosses have poor communication skills. Not all bad communicators are toxic, but if your boss provides vague leadership, withholds information, pits you against your peers, or fosters unhealthy competition between you, they are likely to be toxic.

Toxic bosses are also micromanagers, and want to know what you are doing, when you are doing it, want to see what you are doing, calling and emailing nonstop to keep control over you and your job. They do not trust you, even if you are trustworthy. They assert power and control over you in a very unhealthy way, and this leads to frustration, reduced autonomy, and diminished job satisfaction among staff.

If your boss shows clear favoritism to someone on your team, that is toxic behavior. It makes it difficult to both trust and work with your peers if you feel as though your peer is reporting everything back to your boss. This often causes resentment and division among staff, and teams need to be able to work effectively together, not against each other. I once had a client whose boss called her "stupid" in a meeting, and she told me she has thought about that every day for the last four years. She is not stupid, did nothing stupid, unless you count disagreeing with him stupid. She was mortified, embarrassed, and belittled. That is toxic behavior. He was (and probably still is) a toxic boss.

Bad bosses rarely take responsibility for their mistakes or the problems within the team. Or worse, any wins, accomplishments, or victories, they claim for themselves. True leaders hold themselves accountable for their team's success or failure. Toxic bosses find someone to blame when things go south or expect all the credit when things go well.

I was talking to a young lady, I will call her Maria, who works at a five-star hotel in the U.S. South. After the Covid pandemic, most hospitality venues were having a hard time filling job openings. She had worked there before the pandemic, and when she got called back to work, she was excited to see her friends, co-workers, and customers. Unfortunately, her great, understanding, and kind boss was no longer there. He had been replaced by someone else. She knew on the moment of her arrival, on that very first day, that things were not going to be the same.

Her new female boss, who had previously worked on the hotel's front desk team, had been promoted into a supervisor role. Lacking the right experience and confidence to run a front desk team at a five-star hotel, she immediately began blaming the staff for issues with reservations, customer complaints, and IT system issues—all things that had nothing to do with them. She routinely yelled, berated, and embarrassed the staff, and when things took further turns for the worse, one by one, many of her employees quit or stopped showing up for work.

Maria is a single mother, relies on her paycheck for daycare, housing, and food, so quitting her job was out of the question. She was also within a short driving distance to work, and that was important to her.

So, she stuck with it, and stayed.

Things got progressively worse, and it quickly became apparent that her new boss was not trying nearly hard enough to replace the staff who had left. Maria was working five days a week, staying late, and covering extra shifts. By the end of the second month, she was working six days a week, and getting calls on her one day off to come in and cover or "help out."

By the third month, Maria was working seven days a week. She was leaving her young daughter with a neighbor, and sometimes, she would bring her to work with her when she could not find anyone to babysit.

When her boss reprimanded her for letting her daughter (who was 10 years old), hang out in the employee break room, watching television and playing games on her iPad, Maria told her that she could not leave her daughter alone, and if they needed her to work, she would sometimes have to come with her. Her boss reluctantly relented.

The last time I talked with her, she had worked 71 days in a row without a break or a day off. She was physically, mentally, and emotionally exhausted. I told her that she was between a rock and a hard place. She was beholden to the job, she needed the money, but she would also have to set some boundaries. The hourly staff is not responsible for the failures of the management team. I told her to tell her boss she could only work five days a week, and that if she scheduled her any additional days, she would not be there.

I hope she took my advice and has either found a new job or found some happy medium.

I will share another story with you about a female executive working in the nonprofit space. First, I want to preface this story with a disclaimer. Yes, this was a toxic beyond toxic situation; it was also sexual harassment, which of course, is illegal. So, toxicity in the workplace is unwelcome; and when it crosses the line into what I will describe next, you have protections under the law and should use every resource at your disposal. Those include documenting all harassment, getting HR involved, filing a complaint with the Equal Employment Opportunity Commission (EEOC), and retaining your own attorney as well. Sexual harassment is an actionable offense as well as an illegal one with potential civil and criminal liabilities.

A seasoned marketing executive, she felt fortunate to land a director of marketing position with a nonprofit that she loved, respected, and sincerely believed in its mission. The executive director, a male, was thrilled to have her join the team.

What started off as friendly interaction quickly bypassed any acceptable professional behaviors, and she found herself fending off his advances, ignoring his after-hours calls (which he stated were to chat about work), and on several occasions, she found herself to be the subject of uninvited touching, hugging, and an attempt to give her a backrub at her desk after a particularly long day.

As women often do, she tried to change her behaviors around him to "not lead him on." She often found excuses to not meet with him alone, often bringing her assistant along to "take notes" and provide data. She stopped wearing dresses and heels and started wearing pants and flats. She let it be known that while she was not married, she was in a serious, long-term relationship, and she began chatting about her significant other on a regular basis. It was something she found necessary to do, but it made her quite uncomfortable. She's always been private about her personal life, but she was hoping this information would make him back off.

It did not. When he told her that they would be going to a conference together, she cringed. She instructed her assistant to make sure that her hotel room was on a different floor from his.

A true professional, she felt like she could handle him, and hopefully, deflect or discourage any unwanted attention on their trip. When she arrived at the hotel, she found that their room reservations were next door to each other. After checking in, she went to the front desk to have her room changed and was able to move to a different floor. He was quite surprised to find that when he knocked on her door the next morning to "escort her down to the breakfast meeting," she was not there.

Upon entering the first meeting of the day, he approached her with a curt "good morning" and barely spoke to her the rest of the morning. That afternoon, at a lunch break, he made a joke at her expense. That evening, after dinner, and a few too many drinks, he asked her why she changed her room. She finally told him that he was making her uncomfortable, and she would appreciate it if he would respect her boundaries and keep their working relationship strictly professional.

He told her that "he was just kidding around" and that he's an affectionate guy, as if that was an acceptable answer.

Soon after, he began finding issues with her work. She was over budget, the marketing campaign she was doing on social media to promote their events were "ineffective," and from now on, she would be required to run all of her marketing plans, ideas, and programs by him for approval.

To make a long story short, she quit. When she tried to apply for another job, she'd get called for interviews, but would not get any offers. He was badmouthing her all over the place, and when companies would call for a reference, he instructed the HR team to classify her as "not eligible for rehire."

She filed a complaint with the EEOC, got a lawyer, and last I heard, it was all still pending. But I have a good feeling that she's going to come out on top. During meetings with her attorney, he was able to uncover that she was not the first person from this organization with the same story about the same guy.

Unfortunately, this type of behavior or outcome is not uncommon. Toxicity in the workplace can have long-lasting repercussions, and short of winning a lawsuit, she will probably never work in a nonprofit again. Because she was not willing to play his game, the damage to her reputation and career cannot be quantified or replaced.

Before it gets too far, or past the point of no return, pay close attention to these signs of a toxic boss/toxic workplace.

- Excessive criticism
- Unrealistic expectations
- Lack of recognition
- Bullying and harassment
- Resistance to feedback
- High turnover

It's important to know that working under a toxic boss can have serious effects on your mental and physical well-being. If you are throwing up, having gastrointestinal issues, anxiety, or depression associated with your job, get help. Seek support from HR, go over your boss's head, document all instances of abuse and harassment, and begin exploring options for finding a healthier work environment.

> The foundation of your workplace should be respect, not excuses.

32

Are You HOT?

I have been chasing skinny my entire life.

Except for that ONE time in eleventh grade when I was so stressed out from college applications, SATs, and relationship drama that I forgot to eat and weighed around 110 pounds.

On my 5-foot, 7-inch frame, those pounds made me pretty skinny. It was glorious. I still have one picture taken of me during that time. I should have it framed and mounted on my refrigerator. But other than that, I'm always in a state of "having to lose a few pounds."

If you tune into social media, and who doesn't, it seems like the whole world is skinny, perfect, beautiful. But if you look at the epidemic of weight loss drugs, weight loss diets, weight loss schemes, it seems like everyone is trying to look better.

When I was a kid growing up, there was no such thing as Botox or filler or butt surgeries. If you wanted to be skinny, fit, or look good in your bathing suit, you laid in the sun to get a tan (which immediately knocks off 10 pounds) or you stopped shoving donuts and pizza in your mouth. It was that simple.

But today, we are all chasing youth, beauty, perfection.

In a job search, there is something to it.

Do you know that people who are considered "good looking" or "attractive" get more interviews and job offers?

Yep, it is true. According to a 2021 study at the University of Buffalo, "Attractive people are more likely to get hired, receive better evaluations, and get paid more." But mostly this applies to men.

CEOs tend to be tall, handsome men. So do top-performing sales reps in the white-collar space as well as managers, C-suite executives, and politicians.

So, what do you do if you are not what society considers a "10?"

Well, from someone (me) who is a solid "6" in the looks category, there are ways to make up for your lack of gorgeousness.

People are attracted to attractiveness, but they are also attracted to confidence. The candidate who goes into the job interview knowing the answers, able to project knowledge, confidence, and capability, often comes out on top. Long nose or dad bod notwithstanding.

On the flip side, while beautiful women get more interviews, they get fewer job offers. Why? Because beautiful women are perceived as bitches. Not nice. Or penalized for being pretty.

Head spinning? Yep, mine too. So, are women supposed to be pretty or smart or both?

Yes, to all the above.

I had a female client who worked her way up as an executive in the nonprofit space. She was brilliant, well educated, passionate about helping others, and drop-dead gorgeous. Everywhere she went, her beauty was an attribute in winning the hearts and minds of donors, supporters, and her community partners.

Until it wasn't. She became a target of sexual harassment from a board member, and despite her best efforts at fighting off his advances, he would not back off. He wanted her and did not want to take "no" for an answer. So, she left.

Now, when she interviews, she does so in plain clothing, little makeup, and no fanfare. She's still passionate, just not as true to herself.

Have you ever heard of something called the "halo effect?" The halo effect is a cognitive bias where people assume that if you are attractive, you also possess other desirable qualities such as competence or intelligence.

Of course, that is not true. Not all attractive people are smart, nice, or even social.

Hiring decisions can be absolutely influenced by these unconscious biases. Beautiful people may be seen as a "fit" for a company's image or culture, even if this judgment is not based on qualifications or skills.

There was a well-known effort back in the 1990s by certain pharmaceutical companies to hire very attractive female sales representatives. They would hire them right out of college, train and educate them on products, and turn them loose into territories to go out and win sales.

It was perceived that these young female reps would have a much better chance of capturing the time and attention of the mostly male doctors, who did not have much time in their busy days to see sales representatives. But the idea that they would "stop for a pretty girl" became a prevalent method in increasing market growth, capturing new business, and driving sales.

And, for the most part, it worked.

So, if you are not perfect, not supermodel gorgeous, not skinny, nor fit, nor handsome, can you get a job?

Of course. The real world is much different from the perceived one that we see on television and social media. Real people have jobs; real people make a lot of money; real people are considered happy, successful, and fulfilled.

The most attractive thing that you can have as a candidate, looking for a new job, is confidence. And that confidence comes from your talents, skills, brain power, ideas, drive, passion, and potential. Not your looks.

So, eat that donut, enjoy that slice of pizza, take the day off from the gym without hesitation. You are still you and you are amazing.

> It doesn't matter if you are a "10" on the outside, Strive to be a "10" on the inside.

33 | Mister Rogers

I received a note from a young lady on LinkedIn asking me for some advice. She was seriously struggling in her job search. An HR professional, she'd been ghosted, rejected, and passed over more times than she could count, and really, really needed to land a job. I chatted with her through messages, gave her some job search advice, but the tone of her note had my "mom" radar on high alert. So I got real, really fast. "What's really going on here?" I asked her. Without hesitation, she poured out her heart. "I have a new baby," she told me. "We have no food, no money, and no family in a position to help."

She had been laid off from her previous job. Unemployment had been delayed, and she was down to her last few dollars. So, I said to her, "Let's solve your immediate problem, give me your address, I'm sending you a load of groceries." Within a few hours, I'd ordered up a big delivery of milk, bread, diapers, meat, household items, snacks, and enough food to get her through the next few weeks.

She was dumbfounded. I'm a stranger. She's a stranger. But we are both moms. I've been where she was. A few hundred bucks spent; faith in humanity restored. A month or so later, I received a note from her that she'd just accepted a new position that's going to allow her (and her darling little baby) to not only survive but thrive.

While I like to think I'm a generous person (dropping money in the Salvation Army bucket and making donations to the local food bank), I'm not normally in the habit of sending groceries to strangers. But that day, in that moment, she needed someone and that someone was me.

I know as a society, we are all a bit exhausted by the "tipping" culture, the GoFundMe requests, the worthy causes, the fundraising efforts that inundate us all day long. And that can get tiresome. But if you've been fortunate enough to be born with some common sense, can see through what is real and what is not, and take action . . . youi just never know what a difference you might make.

I say that I live by the "Mister Rogers' philosophy." If you don't know who Mister Rogers is, you should look him up (Fred McFeely Rogers), watch some of the old television shows (*Mister Rogers' Neighborhood*), read about his life and legacy, and try to implement some of his words and thoughts into your words and actions.

Mister Rogers grew up about seven miles from where I did. He was a legend: a local and national celebrity, and the kinds of things you learned about in kindergarten, my generation (Generation X) learned from watching his show on PBS.

Mister Rogers was a beloved personality, educator, and minister, and he hosted the iconic television show *Mister Rogers' Neighborhood*, which aired for over 30 years. He created educational and entertainment programming, and he, along with a talented cast of characters, focused his show, skits, and songs on things like kindness, friendship, acceptance, and emotions. His most famous song, "Won't You Be My Neighbor?" is known across the world as an anthem of love, peace, and acceptance.

In each episode, when he walked through the door, he changed from his suit jacket to a cardigan sweater, signaling that the show was about to begin. He was known for his unwavering kindness, and his messages instilled in us the importance of treating every person with respect and love, regardless of their age, background, or circumstances.

Mister Rogers has many famous quotes, several of which I will share with you, but there is one well-known quote that is not from him, but from his mother. When Mister Rogers was little, and bad things would happen in the world, he would tell his mom that he was scared or anxious or sad about things he had no control over. And she told him, "When you are frightened, look for the helpers. You will always find people who are helping."

That quote has stuck with me throughout my life, and often shapes my actions, words, and deeds.

Obviously, you cannot donate to every charity. You cannot help everyone. But one action, one act of kindness, one donation, or time well spent with someone who needs you is often well within your reach. So, when faced with choice, be the helper.

Or when the world gets you down, look for the helpers. They bring the light, hope, and inspiration that we all need from time to time.

In my business, I am fortunate enough to have a great team around me that runs the day-to-day operations of my business, so I spend most of my time doling out free advice to the hundreds of job seekers that message me on LinkedIn each day.

I am a stranger to them, even though they feel like they know me through my numerous LinkedIn posts.

I try to be encouraging. I sympathize with their situations. I tell them when something is unfair, unethical, or that it is time to move on. I laugh with them over stupid hiring practices. Sometimes I cry with them when life and work is so unfair, or they've been mistreated. Most of all, I listen, provide a kind word or some advice that helps them move past their bad experiences.

I am no angel. I have the mouth of a truck driver—no offense to truck drivers. I get angry, I am impulsive, and sometimes I am irrational. I am a fierce protector of my kids, my staff, and my clients. But despite all of that, I live my life looking for the helpers, trying to be one, and encouraging others to be helpers too.

Here are some of my favorite Mister Rogers' quotes:

- "You are special, and so is your neighbor."
- "It's a beautiful day in the neighborhood."
- "The greatest gift you ever give is your honest self."
- "There's no person in the whole world like you, and I like you just the way you are."

"Listening is where love begins: listening to ourselves and then to our neighbors."

"Knowing that we can be loved exactly as we are gives us all the best opportunity for growing into the healthiest of people."

"Love isn't a state of perfect caring. It is an active noun like *struggle*. To love someone is to strive to accept that person exactly the way he or she is, right here and now."

If you find yourself in a situation, and we all have, where it is so satisfying to yell, complain, and vent our frustrations, try taking a deep breath and thinking about what Mister Rogers might say and do. When you adopt this type of attitude, where most of your words, thoughts, and actions are based on kindness, empathy, and compassion, you make the world a better place. One thought, one word, one action at a time.

> Words matter; be careful how you use yours.

About the Author

Robynn Storey is an accomplished entrepreneur and business leader, widely recognized as the CEO of Storeyline Resumes, a prominent company specializing in professional resume writing and career services. With her unwavering dedication to empowering individuals in their job-search endeavors, Robynn has revolutionized the resume-writing industry and has become a trusted name among professionals worldwide.

Robynn's career journey is a testament to her exceptional expertise in the field. After completing her education in business administration, she embarked on a mission to bridge the gap between job seekers and their dream careers. Recognizing the importance of a compelling resume in the competitive job market, she founded Storeyline Resumes with a vision to provide top-notch resume writing services that showcase each client's unique skills and experiences.

Under Robynn's dynamic leadership, Storeyline Resumes has emerged as a premier destination for individuals seeking professional resume assistance. With a keen understanding of industry trends and employer expectations, Robynn and her team have crafted hundreds of thousands of resumes that have opened doors to new opportunities for countless professionals. Her commitment to delivering excellence has earned Storeyline Resumes a reputation for providing tailored, attention-grabbing resumes that effectively highlight the strengths of each client.

Robynn's passion for empowering job seekers extends beyond resume writing. She has spearheaded the development of comprehensive career services at Storeyline Resumes, offering interview coaching, LinkedIn profile optimization, and career counseling to ensure individuals are well equipped to navigate the competitive job market. Robynn believes in a holistic approach to career development, and her dedication to her clients' success sets Storeyline Resumes apart as a trusted resource for comprehensive career support.

In addition to her role at Storeyline Resumes, Robynn is a sought-after speaker and thought leader, frequently sharing her insights and expertise at industry conferences, podcasts, and events. She is known for her dynamic presentations on resume writing, personal branding, and career advancement, captivating audiences with her deep knowledge and engaging speaking style.

Beyond her professional accomplishments, Robynn has always been an unwavering advocate for empowering women and families. Her team works remotely, and she encourages all staff to put their families first, while having the ability to earn a lucrative living on their own terms and timelines.

Robynn Storey's remarkable leadership as the CEO of Storeyline Resumes has redefined the resume-writing industry and empowered countless individuals to achieve their career goals. Her commitment to excellence, innovative approach, and dedication to client success make her a true trailblazer in the field.

With over a million followers on LinkedIn, her posts on advocacy for job seekers, no-holds-barred approach to improve the job seeker experience, and unwavering support for respect and open communication between employers and job seekers, get viewed by over 200 million people annually from across the globe.

Index